BUSINESS PLANS FOR FILMMAKERS

Business Plans for Filmmakers

John W. Cones

Southern Illinois University Press
Carbondale and Edwardsville

13 12 11 10   4 3 2 1

Library of Congress Cataloging-in-Publication Data
Cones, John W.
 Business plans for filmmakers / John W. Cones.
      p. cm.
 Includes bibliographical references and index.
 ISBN-13: 978-0-8093-2994-6 (pbk. : alk. paper)
 ISBN-10: 0-8093-2994-8 (pbk. : alk. paper)
 ISBN-13: 978-0-8093-8583-6 (e-book)
 ISBN-10: 0-8093-8583-X (e-book)
 1. Motion pictures—Production and direction.
 2. Motion picture industry—Finance. 3. Business
 planning. I. Title.
 PN1995.9.P7C66 2010
 384'.83—dc22   2010004939

Printed on recycled paper. ♻
The paper used in this publication meets the minimum requirements of American National Standard
for Information Sciences—Permanence of Paper for
Printed Library Materials, ANSI Z39.48-1992. ∞

Contents

Introduction

Considered from a broad perspective, this book is written for a fairly customary reason: to fill a perceived gap in the film-industry literature. More specifically, however, the existence of this gap is primarily due to a failure on the part of business-plan consultants, entertainment attorneys and film-industry association executives to provide the independent-film community with adequate and accurate information relating to the proper role of business plans in film finance. The sad truth is that the use of business plans has been oversold to the independent-film community. Many of the people involved have consistently perpetuated numerous myths and served as sources of misinformation regarding the legitimate use of business plans, some for self-serving reasons but others for a simple lack of knowledge and understanding. The following statements represent such myths:

1. One of the first things to do when seeking to finance a feature or documentary film is to prepare a business plan.
2. A business plan is useful in seeking film finance from film-industry sources.
3. The primary means for raising money to produce a film from investors outside of the film industry is through the use of a business plan.
4. A business plan can be used by itself to raise money from investors.
5. A business plan may be used to raise money from passive investors.
6. A business plan is just another name for a private-placement offering memorandum (i.e., a business plan and a PPM are the same thing).
7. Even if one needs to use a private-placement offering memorandum, one should also use a business plan as supplementary material.
8. Even if one needs a securities disclosure document, it will be helpful to the securities attorney for the filmmaker to have already prepared a business plan first.

Each of these statements is false and misleading. This book elaborates on the reasons why these statements are false, but here are the corresponding short responses:

1. It depends on the type of film finance being pursued. A business plan is not useful or appropriate for many forms of film finance including certain forms of investor financing.[1]
2. Industry financing sources such as the major studios, their affiliated distribution companies, other established production companies and most entertainment lenders do not need to see a business plan; rather, a producer's package provides the appropriate level of documentation for them (see discussion regarding the producer's package in chapter 1).
3. A business plan's usefulness in helping to raise money is limited to one to a few fairly rare active investors from outside the industry, people many producers do not want to be involved with their films for the very fact that they will be actively involved in helping make the important management decisions associated with the project (see the discussion regarding the differences between active and passive investors and why that distinction is important in chapter 1).
4. A business plan is not an investment vehicle and therefore must be paired with an investment vehicle that is suitable for use with active investors (see discussion regarding investment vehicles that may be appropriately used with active investors in chapter 1).[2]
5. A business plan cannot be legally used by itself to raise money from passive investors but may serve as supplemental material to a properly drafted securities disclosure document, although risks are involved in using business plans as supplemental material when seeking to raise money from passive investors (see discussion in chapter 1).
6. Business plans and securities disclosure documents are two different documents with some similar and overlapping content but also some different content, and the two have distinctively different uses (see chapter 1).
7. Using any supplemental material including a separate business plan with a private-placement-offering memorandum in a private offering of securities is accompanied by a certain level of additional risk (see discussion of overly aggressive business-plan consultant tactics below).
8. This may be good advice for a young and inexperienced securities attorney or one with little to no experience putting together a film private-placement-offering memorandum, but for a securities attorney with considerable experience putting together film offerings, only a small percentage of the information put into a business plan will be useful,

and that will likely have to be carefully edited. The better practice is to just provide the limited and selected information requested by the securities attorney, not a full business plan.

Notwithstanding the possibility that a business plan might be a useful planning tool for any business, including a film-production company, the primary reason why most filmmakers get involved with business plans is their desire to raise money for a project from investors. Thus, the focus of this book is on using business plans to actually raise money to develop, produce or distribute a feature or documentary motion picture. Using a business plan for planning purposes has been dealt with adequately in other books about more-generic business plans.

So many definitions. As suggested by the above discussion, one of the first problems encountered by any business person or more specifically a filmmaker for purposes of this book who is thinking about creating a business plan is that the phrase "business plan" has so many different meanings, and business plans are used for many different purposes. So, it is important for a book of this type and the people thinking about drafting a business plan to focus on the kind of business plan actually being discussed and the purpose for which it is intended to be used.

In a very general sense, a business plan is a written statement of goals for a business venture. It may also contain a discussion of why such goals are appropriate, how they may be achieved, how the business is organized, who is involved with the business, how the business relates to the existing marketplace and, in the case of for-profit enterprises, some information relating to its prospects for financial success.

Another definition of a business plan sees it as any plan that helps a business to look forward, allocate its resources, focus on key issues and prepare to handle anticipated problems and opportunities. That is a rather broad definition of a business plan and includes the business plans that are drafted primarily for the purpose of serving as a guide for a business's operations, as opposed to raising money from investors.

At another level, a business plan may be created for a nonprofit or a for-profit venture. These broad differences in the orientation of the business are reflected in the written statement referred to as a business plan. That orientation, of course, tends to have an impact on the choices made relating to the kinds of information to include in the business plan. The nonprofit ventures tend to focus on the services to be provided, whereas the for-profit ventures tend to focus on the prospects for making a profit for the business and its investors.

Certain kinds of business plans also may have a more-narrow focus. For example, some are drafted for the limited purpose of changing the public's perception of a particular product or service. Those business plans may be more commonly referred to as marketing plans. They are primarily used for marketing purposes. Choices relating to the contents of such a business plan will relate directly to its overall purpose. The contents of other business plans differ because they are being created for a different purpose. The contents of a business plan must be consistent with and match the specific purpose for which the business plan is intended.

Another way to look at a business plan that may also significantly impact the choices relating to its contents is whether this written statement is primarily being prepared for use by an internal or external audience. In other words, some business plans are primarily written as guides for a company's employees to help keep them on track and all moving toward the same goals. These business plans tend to focus on the business goals and its philosophy. Other business plans are primarily written for the purpose of raising money from outsiders. These tend to focus on the backgrounds and experience of the management team, the competitive marketplace and financial projections.

The contents of a business plan intended for use as a means for raising money from outside sources also vary depending on whether the business plan is presented to prospective lenders or investors. Lenders want to know about the assets of the business, whether there is any existing collateral and about the prospects for the ability of the business to pay back a proposed loan with interest in a timely manner. Outside investors are more interested in seeing information relating to the prospects for financial success of the venture.

Still another distinction between business plans is based on whether the plan is being used to raise money for a company or for a project. Organizational structures differ between these two types of business plans; thus, the statements made in the business plan vary. A company-oriented business plan tends to favor long-term business goals and the corporate structure. As discussed more fully later, the business plan can only appropriately be used with a corporation to be formed upon funding, not in selling the shares of an existing corporation. That requires a securities offering including a securities disclosure document, not a business plan.

On the other hand, project financing (e.g., a single motion picture or a slate of films) tends to be structured using limited-term investment vehicles. For the active investor, that includes the investor financing agreement, the joint-venture agreement or the member-managed limited liability company (LLC). The passive-investor investment vehicles that require a securities disclosure document include the limited partnership and the manager-managed LLC.[3]

This book is not intended to discuss all varieties of the business plan. Its focus, once again, is more narrow. The emphasis here is on the for-profit venture, specifically relating to feature or documentary films, on seeking outside financing as opposed to internal planning and coordination and more about limited-term project financing from outside investors as opposed to long-term company or lender financing. Further, as discussed in more detail later, in order to meet certain legal requirements, the outside investors targeted by the filmmaker's business plan discussed here must be actively involved in the venture's management (i.e., passive investors trigger securities' law-compliance obligations). Despite the best efforts of some business-plan consultants to confuse or overpromote the utility of the business plan for film finance, the business plan's legitimate use is limited to raising money through several specific investment vehicles and only from a few active investors (see additional requirements of the active investor in chapter 1).

To make it even more difficult for aspiring filmmakers, most of the other available books about business plans appear to focus on the corporation as the investment vehicle and do not make the important distinction between corporations to be formed, as opposed to the existing corporation. Further, other books often emphasize using the business plan as a planning tool or as a means for seeking lender financing from external sources. Neither of these approaches is that useful to a filmmaker, and using a book or a model business plan with such an orientation can not only be confusing but can actually do more harm than good, because the more language that is borrowed from a business plan that is not on target with respect to a filmmaker's specific choice of investment vehicle or the business plan's purpose, the more confusing that language will be to prospective investors. Thus, filmmakers need to be forewarned about using the wrong book about business plans or using the wrong sample business plan as a model.

Business-plan consultants. Another problem area that filmmakers need to be aware of—the overly aggressive business-plan consultant. Unfortunately, the film industry has for many years attracted some less than ethical individuals, particularly in this field of film finance. Some of these less than ethical individuals come in the guise of business-plan consultants who use several different tactics to take undeserved fees from filmmakers.

One of these tactics is to confuse filmmakers about the appropriate time to use a business plan. That is why this book takes the time to carefully explain when it is appropriate to use a business plan and when it is not. These business-plan consultants tend to preach that the business plan is the first and most important step in obtaining financing for a feature or documentary film. As noted above, that is not actually true. As explained in more detail as this book moves forward, the business plan actually has very limited use in the field of film finance.

Another misconception often put forth by some business-plan consultants is that it is a good idea or even required that a business plan be prepared and used in conjunction with a securities disclosure document (e.g., a PPM) when raising money from a group of passive investors. In addition to being redundant, such supplemental use of a business plan (i.e., material used to supplement a PPM) is risky because it may contain statements that are false or misleading (i.e., not reviewed by the securities attorney) and when used with a securities disclosure document, may make the film producer vulnerable to charges of fraud even if the securities disclosure document was drafted pursuant to the law.

Often, securities attorneys are contracted to be paid by the hour, so if an independent producer has the extra money necessary to pay a securities attorney to review the producer's business plan, as well as prepare the securities disclosure document to make sure they are both consistent with each other and the law, that may work out. In my experience, of course, independent-film producers usually do not have the extra money to waste. Further, in those instances where the securities attorney has agreed to prepare the securities disclosure document (and handle associated tasks) on a flat-fee basis, it is unreasonable to also ask him or her to review a separate business plan in addition, unless that specific additional task has been negotiated up front, specifically included in the engagement letter as one of the tasks to be performed by the attorney and included in the overall price for the job. In any case, the better practice is to use a marketing brochure with text already approved by the securities attorney, instead of using a full business plan to supplement a securities disclosure document.

Another tactic used by such business-plan consultants is to promote themselves as the preparer of a business plan that resulted in a highly successful movie, thus implying that if the filmmaker uses this same business-plan consultant to prepare a business plan, that increases the likelihood that the film will be a success. This tactic is used throughout the film industry by many people in addition to some business-plan consultants, and it is equally false in each case. Film finance and film production are both collaborative processes (i.e., a lot of people may be involved). In any given instance, it is difficult at best to determine who made the most significant contributions to the box-office success of a given movie or that any given individual is even competent in a particular field simply because he or she was involved with a movie that subsequently did well. In any case, it is simply wrong to assume that because a person was associated with a successful movie in some way, that their contribution was valuable. If all of the subsequent film producers who used that business-plan consultant's services were not as successful, that suggests the business plan for the highly successful movie had little to do with the movie's subsequent success.

Furthermore, if a business plan associated with a successful movie was used to raise money from a group of passive investors without the use of a securities disclosure document, the financing of such a movie project would have actually been illegal. Just because they may have gotten away with it does not make it right. Someone who is careless in knowing when it is proper to use a business plan and when it is not is not someone a filmmaker wants on his or her film-finance team.

Finally, another way to mislead their potential customers, some business-plan consultants write books that have overly broad titles. In other words, a book title that suggests it is about film finance generally when, in fact, it is limited to a discussion of film business plans only is quite misleading because the use of business plans in film finance is such a small part of the broader field of film finance. Of course, book titles are often suggested by the book publishers and not the authors, but that's when the book's author has to exercise some ethical standards by disapproving of such an overly broad and misleading book title.

What a filmmaker must know. Filmmakers must know when it is appropriate and when it is not appropriate to use a business plan. They must know which of a limited number of available investment vehicles are appropriately paired with a business plan. They must know in what ways a business plan is similar to a securities disclosure document and in what ways these two documents differ. They must know the difference between company financing and project financing. All of these issues help determine the specific language to be used in drafting the business plan. This book addresses each of these important issues.

A review of this book's table of contents shows that it follows a rather traditional outline for a business plan. Unfortunately, the traditional main headings for business plans do not always work for film-related business plans, particularly when the business plan and associated investment vehicle are being used to raise funds for project financing, as opposed to company financing. For that reason, one or more of the early paragraphs in each chapter discuss other possible titles for the main sections of a business plan being used for project financing associated with film projects or phases in the life of a film.

Examples of business-plan sections. Accompanying each chapter are examples of the various sections and subsections discussed in that chapter. Note that these examples do not come from a single source (i.e., one integrated business plan or securities disclosure document). They have been borrowed from a number of different business plans and securities disclosure documents to illustrate the particular point being made in that chapter. For that reason, the language may reflect that an investor financing agreement is the investment vehicle, another reflecting a member-managed LLC as the investment vehicle and so on. Other examples may have been taken from development offerings or production offerings. Some may be for a single film while others are for multiple film slates. When borrowing from the examples, it is important that the filmmaker understand which investment vehicle is being used with his or her business plan, if any; whether the business plan is being used to raise money for development, production or distribution; whether the business plan is for a single motion picture or a slate of films; and how to change the language in the example to be consistent with these choices.[4]

In addition, most of the charts included in the business-plan sample sections are provided for illustrative purposes only. In each instance, it will be necessary for a preparer of a business plan in the years ahead to update each chart. It may be possible to go back to the source cited in the example and to find similar information for the current year, although Web sites do change, and the contents may or may not be the same each year.

This book is designed to encourage (without pushing toward one choice or the other) the filmmaker to think through the process and to understand what the choices are and what the advantages and disadvantages may be. Is the business plan for a development, production or distribution deal? Long-term company financing or for project financing? A single film or a multiple film slate? A documentary or feature? An investor financing agreement, joint venture agreement, a corporation to be formed or a member-managed LLC? This is the most likely way for a filmmaker to end up with a business plan that actually fits his or her filmmaking needs.

1. Preliminary Considerations

The first of several important preliminary considerations for a filmmaker think-ing about preparing a business plan is to determine whether he or she really needs a business plan or not. Unfortunately, filmmakers are often advised to create a business plan to help them raise money, even when a business plan may not be appropriate. In all fairness, the business plan is not a financing vehicle or entity, and investors cannot invest in a business plan or buy shares in a business plan. However, a business plan can be used in conjunction with several other investor-financing techniques to raise money for film projects. For example, a business plan can be used with an investor-financing agreement to raise money from a single active investor. It can be used with a joint-venture agreement to raise money from another entity also acting as an active investor / joint-venture partner. It can also be used as a means of identifying possible founding shareholders for the initial incorporation or the initial member-managers of a member-managed limited-liability company (LLC).[1]

Business Plan or Securities Disclosure Document

Based on numerous conversations with producers of independent feature films, there appears to be a considerable amount of misunderstanding and/or misinfor-mation in the film community regarding when to use a business plan as opposed to a securities-disclosure document if seeking to raise money from investors to develop, produce or distribute one or more independent feature films.

First, the filmmaker needs to understand what a business plan is and how it differs from a securities-disclosure document. Although there may be similari-ties (i.e., some overlap with respect to the contents), these two documents are not the same thing. The differences are based on both the contents of these two documents as well as in the appropriate uses of them.

A business plan is a written statement that describes and analyzes a business (in this particular case, a proposed independently produced feature-length movie) and gives detailed projections about the future of that business. Again, a business plan is not an investment vehicle, and shares in a business plan cannot be sold. Nobody can invest in a business plan. If a business plan is used to actually raise money, it must be combined with an appropriate investment vehicle but only in limited circumstances, that is, to raise money from one, two or a few active investors. A business plan cannot be appropriately used to actually raise money from a larger group of passive investors, except institutional investors (organizations that regularly trade large volumes of securities such as mutual funds, banks, insurance companies, pension funds, labor-union funds, corporate profit-sharing plans and college endowment funds).

Active versus passive investors. Unfortunately, for small businesses throughout the country, this line between active and passive investors is not all that clear. Securities regulations do not provide either a specific number of investors beyond which it is impossible for all of them to be considered active, nor do such regulations provide definitive guidance about how much activity is enough, what kind of activity is active and to what extent the investor must be qualified in order to be considered actively involved.

This lack of specifics is unfortunate because the risks are significant. If the promoter of a business venture uses a business plan to raise money from some undefined number of active investors, but these investors fail to qualify as active investors (or there are simply too many of them for all of them to be actively involved), that promoter of the business venture may be guilty of selling an unregistered security and subject to both civil and criminal penalties. Such a business promoter is very likely to be guilty of selling an unregistered security because he or she did not even recognize that he or she was selling a security and, as a consequence, made no attempt to register the transaction with the U.S. Securities and Exchange Commission (SEC) at the federal level and with the securities regulatory authorities in each state where sales were contemplated, as required by law. Nor would the promoter have even attempted to otherwise comply with all of the conditions and limitations imposed on the use of any of the available exemptions from the securities-registration requirement (i.e., a private placement).

The difference between an active and a passive investor is that an active investor is regularly involved in helping the filmmaker make important decisions with respect to the film. That means helping to select the script, making changes in the script, selecting the director and lead actors, choosing the line producer and director of photography, helping to solve problems that come up during production, helping to make decisions relating to distribution and so forth. These one, two or a few active investors need to be capable of making valuable contributions on these important questions—they need to have some knowledge of and experience in the film industry that is relevant to what the filmmaker is doing and be actively involved in helping to make such decisions on a regular basis. That does not mean they should have veto power, although some investors who put in most of the money to produce a film, for example, may insist on such control, and in that instance, it may become a problem for a producer.

In addition, unless an entity is created to provide limited liability, active investors may not have the limited-liability protection offered by such an entity; most people with enough money to invest a substantial amount in a high-risk venture such as an independent film will most likely prefer to enjoy limited-liability protection. That is just another factor to consider when determining whether to use a business plan and seek financing from one, two or a few active investors.

A passive investor is someone who is not an active investor (i.e., someone who is not regularly involved in helping to make those important decisions). This is an important distinction because it represents the essence of the difference between a nonsecurities offering and a securities offering. Essentially, anytime a filmmaker is seeking to raise money from one or more passive investors, he or she is selling a security, no matter what he or she calls it. So, the producer's decision to raise money from active or passive investors has important implications and consequences.

Authoritative court cases provide further guidance. It is clear, that it is not enough that the filmmaker choose one of the four so-called active-investor investment vehicles, the investors have to be active in fact and be qualified to participate. The pivotal criterion for distinguishing partnership or joint-venture interests as well as limited-liability-company interests that are securities from those that are not usually will be the question of whether the investors have an expectation of profits based substantially on the efforts of others. Where profits are expected to come substantially from the efforts of others (as is typical with a limited partnership or a manager-managed LLC), the courts will treat that as a security. On the other hand, where profits are expected to come from the joint efforts of partners (the typical case in a general partnership, joint venture or a member-managed LLC), the courts are not likely to consider that arrangement a security (thus the concepts of the active investor and the active-investor investment vehicle).[2]

The leading case on when a general-partnership interest (and by analogy a joint venture or a member-managed LLC) constitutes a security is the 1981 case of *Williamson v. Tucker*.[3] In the *Williamson* case, the federal Fifth Circuit Court of Appeals said that a general partnership or joint-venture interest may be designated as a security if the investor can establish, for example, that:

Documented authority. An agreement among the parties leaves so little power in the hands of the partner or venturer that the arrangement in fact distributes power as would a limited partnership; or

Knowledge and experience. The partner or venturer is so inexperienced and unknowledgeable in business affairs that he or she is incapable of intelligently exercising his or her partnership or venture powers; or

Unique managerial activity. The partner or venturer is so dependent on some unique entrepreneurial or managerial ability of the promoter or manager that he or she cannot replace the manager of the enterprise or otherwise exercise meaningful partnership or venture powers.

According to the *Williamson* case, the focus of the current analysis must be on the investor's expectations at the time of the original investment.

Further, California courts have supported the securities regulators' view that an active investor must have some level of knowledge and understanding of the field in which he or she is investing. In the case of *Consolidated Management Group LLC vs. the California Department of Corporations*, a California appellate court ruled that "the investor's inexperience and dependence on a managing venturer served to establish that the joint venture interests were in fact securities." The court further stated that these business promoters (selling investments in oil-well drilling equipment and using a joint venture as the investment vehicle) "were soliciting investments from people who would, as a practical matter, lack the knowledge to effectively exercise the managerial powers conferred by the joint venture agreements. . . . [T]he success of the particular projects marketed was uniquely dependent on the efforts of the . . . managing venturer, and that investors would be relying on those efforts in making their investments." Ultimately, the court observed that the "investments were solicited from persons with no experience in the oil and gas industry."[4] For purposes of this book, we can substitute "general partnership" or "member-managed LLC" for the "joint venture" and "film industry" for the "oil and gas industry."

Note that the *Consolidated Management* case decided in California went beyond the requirement that an investor must be experienced and knowledgeable in business affairs generally, and the case cited with approval a line of cases from the Federal Courts' Fifth, Ninth and Eleventh Circuits that take into account the reality that general business sophistication does not necessarily equip an investor to manage a specialized enterprise. These cases[5] have found, "Regardless of investors' general business experience, where they are inexperienced in the particular business they are likely to be relying solely on the efforts of the promoters to obtain their profits."

The California case *Consolidated Management* was a bit of an easy call for a couple of reasons. First, the company took the position that it was selling a security for federal purposes, since they actually prepared and distributed a private-placement-offering memorandum, not a business plan. They would have been more consistent if they had taken the position that what they were selling was not a security and to have used a business plan to provide information to investors, not a PPM (not that this choice would really matter; they, in fact, were still selling a security). Secondly, the company offered a total of 216 joint-venture interests, and in all fairness, no reasonable person could possibly believe or argue that 100 to 200 investors could be managed in a manner that would allow all of them to be actively involved.

The more difficult questions for the purposes of this book about business plans for filmmakers are:

- What if the filmmaker (business-venture promoter) used a business plan (not a PPM) and only sought to raise money from one to three active investors who were fairly sophisticated business persons but who did not have experience or specialized knowledge about the film industry?
- Assuming the management arrangement otherwise met the criteria of the *Williamson* case, would the facts that the investment is for the film industry and that people and investors generally have more knowledge about films than they do about drilling equipment make a difference?
- What if the filmmaker's business plan contains a well-written Motion Picture Industry Overview that explains to the prospective investor how the film industry works? Does that help meet the knowledge part of the test?
- And since most people with experience and knowledge of the film industry are currently working in the film industry, and they do not need to see a business plan (but, rather, a producer's package, which includes the script, budget, chain-of-title documents [evidence of copyright], information relating to the elements attached to the project and evidence of attachments [the latter being documents showing that actors and director are committed to work on the film project], will be sufficient), does this mean there is no place for using a business plan except for prospective investors who have knowledge and experience in the film industry but who no longer work in the film industry (a very limited number of prospective investors indeed)?

We really don't know how the courts would deal with what we might consider these hypothetical questions. But, if some leeway is not available on the investor-experience issue, then capital formation for small businesses all across the country has been dealt a devastating blow, a result that runs counter to the stated position of the securities regulators, who repeatedly have claimed they are trying to help make it easier for small businesses to raise capital. On the other hand, if a filmmaker finds him- or herself bumping up against any of the above-described circumstances, he or she is close to the edge or has crossed the line into noncompliance.

The more conservative view of the position of the courts and securities regulators (as reflected in the above-cited line of cases) appears to be that no small-businessperson (not just filmmakers) can seek to raise money from even a few active investors unless those investors have knowledge and experience in the subject industry. Of course, that might mean that an entrepreneur who made billions in the computer industry would not be able to become an active investor/executive producer in a film deal and use his or her investment as a way to learn about the movie business unless the filmmaker/promoter structured the deal as a security and used a PPM instead of a business plan to inform the investor. In the alternative, such a wealthy investor could self-fund his or her own production company. These court-imposed rules also mean that no filmmaker can legitimately use a business plan to raise money from prospective active investors outside of the film industry unless the investor has developed his or her specialized knowledge and experience about the film industry in some other way.

As a consequence of these cases, if there is any doubt about how active the investors are going to be or whether they have knowledge and experience in the film industry, it would clearly be safer to structure the deal as a passive investment and use a PPM instead of a business plan. On the other hand, if the filmmaker was willing to allow the investors to be very active, to limit the number of investors to a minimal number (e.g., one, two or three), to inform them about how the film industry operates and/or to only raise money from active investors with experience and knowledge of the film industry, it may be permissible to continue to use a business plan to solicit such investors. The cases, however, seem to permit only a very narrow window for such activities.

Inadvertent felonies. One major concern that is clearly raised by these cases is that a huge gap or disconnect appears to exist between what the law says one can do with respect to active investors and what an entire community of business-plan consultants and others are telling filmmakers and other small-business entrepreneurs what is permissible. Through these cases, the courts and securities-law regulators are saying that the circumstances are extremely limited under which active investors may be solicited with a business plan in order to raise funding for any small-business enterprise. On the other hand, many of the hundreds of business-plan consultants who advise their clients and write about this issue in online articles and books, along with instructors at graduate business schools and film schools, appear to be leading current and future business entrepreneurs to believe that the business plan is the key to raising money from investors, without even discussing the distinction between active and passive investors, much less how limited the active-investor opportunity is. This all suggests that most of the thousands of small-business entrepreneurs and filmmakers who are using business plans every year to raise money for their business enterprises or projects are breaking the law, and they do not even know it.

If that is the situation, business-plan consultants all across the country need to talk to their securities attorneys, securities regulators and legislators and seek both clarification of the government's policy and further reduction in their clients' capital-formation burden. Otherwise, this significant disconnect will continue between the law and the advice regularly provided by business-plan consultants on raising money using a business plan; and the specter of actions being taken by securities-law enforcement against independent filmmakers and other small-business persons will be a concern.

If a filmmaker is really trying to raise money from one, two or a few active investors who are both capable of being regularly involved in helping to make important decisions and willing to be so involved, he or she can use a business plan (combined with an appropriate investment vehicle) to provide them with the information on which to base their decision. But, if a filmmaker is raising money from one or more passive investors (other than the institutional investors noted above), he or she is required by law to provide those investors with a properly prepared securities-disclosure document (not a business plan) prior to their investment.

In addition, a business plan being used to raise money from one, two or a few active investors should not suggest in any way that the filmmaker is really seeking to raise money from passive investors. Either leave out the discussion about the specific financial arrangements or, at the very least, avoid references to interests in limited partnerships or units in a manager-managed (passive-investor) LLC or shares in an existing corporation.

The language in a business plan should not suggest or imply that the investor will not be permitted to be regularly involved in helping to make important decisions, since that is at the very heart of what makes him or her an active investor. It may be the better practice to actually state that the business plan is being used in conjunction with one of those specific but appropriate investment vehicles for the purpose of raising funds from one, two or a few active investors. In any case, absolutely do not include language that the filmmaker either plans to create or may later create a limited partnership or manager-managed LLC, because that language clearly indicates that the filmmaker is planning a securities offering. Also, do not suggest by the language in the business plan that the intention is to raise money from more than a few active investors, because at some undefined point, it is no longer possible to keep a large number of investors "actively" involved in a business venture in a meaningful way, and if one of the investors is passive, the interest sold is a security.

Active-investor vehicles. The investment vehicles that can appropriately be used in conjunction with a business plan for seeking funds from one, two or a few active investors are, as already mentioned:

- the investor-financing agreement, which may state the revenue-sharing ratio as between the producer/management team and the investor(s)
- the joint-venture agreement, or domestic coproduction, which may state the revenue-sharing deal
- the initial incorporation, formed as either a regular C corporation or an S corporation, limits the revenues to be paid to investor/shareholders to dividends determined strictly in accordance with the percentage ownership of certain classes of stock
- a member-managed (active-investor) LLC, which, in addition to the filing with secretary of state, must have an LLC operating agreement in order to be properly formed. This vehicle may provide a bit more flexibility in structuring the revenue-sharing deal in accordance with the LLC's operating agreement.[6]

Note that selling shares in an existing corporation and selling units in a limited partnership or manager-managed LLC are not included in this list because shares in an existing corporation and units in either a limited partnership or a manager-managed LLC are all securities. For these investment vehicles, the business plan is not the appropriate document to use for providing information to prospective investors. Such offerings require a securities disclosure document (see discussion about the differences between a business plan and a securities disclosure document).

The most commonly presumed advantage of seeking one or a few active investors to fund a film project is the expectation that a filmmaker does not have to pursue as many individual prospects. A filmmaker hopes to get all the money needed in just a few places. Because some of these active investors may actually be quite helpful and knowledgeable, a filmmaker may be able to use that experience to produce a better film or make more-advantageous deals.

Some disadvantages to seeking funds from active investors are that the active investors may interfere with the filmmaker's creative control, the investment vehicle chosen may not offer any limited-liability protection to the active investors, it may be more difficult to find prospective investors who are both capable of and willing to be a lead investor in a high-risk investment like independent film, and the more active investors, the more likely it is that some will actually be passive. It is also important to recognize that by seeking active-investor financing, a filmmaker is eliminating at least two of the advantages of a securities offering (i.e., spreading the risk amongst a larger group of passive investors, none of whom will typically be hurt too badly if they do not get their money back or make a profit, and, of course, passive investors do not interfere with the filmmaker's creative control).

Disclosure-document terminology. A quick note about terminology. The term "securities disclosure document" is a broad term that applies to the required written information that must be provided to prospective investors before they invest in most securities offerings. The terms "prospectus" and "offering circular" are used to describe the securities disclosure documents associated with various types of public/registered offerings. These securities offerings are usually too expensive, complicated and time-consuming to be of much interest to low-budget independent filmmakers. The private-placement-offering memorandum is the term used to describe the securities disclosure document associated with an exempt/private offering, and this is the securities disclosure document most commonly used by low-budget indie filmmakers.

Specific rules promulgated by the SEC and, in some instances, state securities regulatory authorities provide guidance on what information must be disclosed in these securities disclosure documents and how that information must be presented. There are no such rules for business plans, and that is why there is such a wide disparity in the contents of business plans and why the contents of business plans are always different in some respects from the contents of a securities disclosure document, even though some elements of the two are the same or similar.

Specific uses of business plans. Another important use of the business plan is in helping to establish a relationship with prospective investors for a possible subsequent privately placed securities offering.[7] In this sense, the business plan becomes a method for conducting a general solicitation while looking for active investors, and if the active-investor campaign does not prove successful, then the campaign, after a several-week waiting period, can be converted into a securities offering (seeking passive investors). If the *private-placement* approach is used for the subsequent securities offering, those persons contacted during the active-investor general solicitation (using the business plan) may be approached as prospective investors for the private placement. That is because the initial contact with those prospective investors is likely to be sufficient to establish the preexisting relationship, which, although not technically required by the federal securities laws, still is an important element in proving that no general solicitation occurred during the period in which the securities offering was being conducted as an exempt/private offering.

The business plan, however, is not all that useful for seeking financing from studio or other industry sources. Industry professionals are more interested in a producer's package. As a general rule, a business plan is more useful for approaching financing sources outside of the film industry (limited by securities-law considerations). At least that is the case when approaching prospective financing sources who are already involved in the film industry—a business plan is not needed; a producer's package will do. In addition, a business plan is not appropriate for use in seeking to raise money from a large group of passive investors because that activity tends to involve the sale of a security, and a securities disclosure document is required.

To help clarify the relationships among specific sources of film financing and the type of documentation that is most appropriate, and in some cases legally required, figure 1.1 illustrates the basic documentation with which to approach various film financing sources:

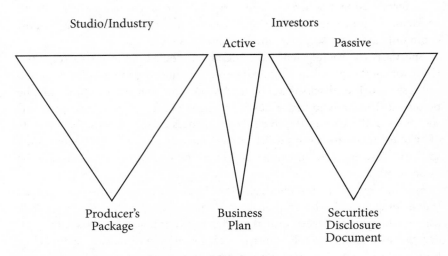

Figure 1.1. Documentation for sources of film finance.

Note that in figure 1.1, the world of film finance, represented by the horizontal line, is divided into two major segments: studio/industry financing and investor financing. Studio/industry financing includes the production-financing/distribution deal, negative pickup transactions, foreign presales, gap financing and joint ventures with industry partners, along with domestic and international coproductions. Each of these forms of film finance is most appropriately approached with a producer's package, not a business plan or securities disclosure document. The form of film finance that does not require a producer's package is the in-house development/production/distribution deal, which is usually sought solely with a pitch of a movie concept, and which occurs well before the producer's package is created.[8]

The investor-financing side comprises active investors and passive investors. The active investors are most appropriately approached with a business plan accompanied by an active-investor investment vehicle. The passive investors are required by law to be approached with a securities disclosure document.

Another way to present the same information is the following listing of the sources for film finance and the documentation with which to approach that financing source.

Source of Production Financing	Appropriate Documentation
major studio/distributor	producer's package
film-production company	producer's package
entertainment lender	producer's package and distribution deal
commercial lender	business plan and description of collateral
a few active investors (outside the industry)	business plan and investment vehicle
passive investors	securities disclosure document

As noted above, a producer's package is typically not bound and might consist of the film's script, evidence of copyrights (chain of title documents), information relating to the elements attached to the project and the proposed budget. A business plan, on the other hand, is typically a bit more organized (i.e., bound with a table of contents) and will generally include a synopsis of the script (but not the entire script), chain of title documents as exhibits, information relating to the attached elements (e.g., narrative biographies of the people committed to the project), a summary of the budget and other information discussed in this book. A business plan can be as simple or as sophisticated as the producer and his or her advisers choose to make it. The securities disclosure document may include all of the information normally found in a business plan (edited more rigorously to avoid fraud) plus information required to be disclosed to prospective investors by the applicable federal or state securities laws (e.g., tax discussion, tax opinion, securities opinion, risk factors, and the like).

The documentation for investor-financing transactions is different from the investment vehicle. Unfortunately, some authors writing about business plans have confused the two. The business plan with one of the four active-investor investment vehicles may be useful in seeking to raise money from one to a few active investors. But if a passive-investor investment vehicle is preferred because the money is being sought from a group of passive investors, then the passive-investor investment vehicles are appropriate (i.e., limited partnership, manager-managed LLC or an existing corporation), and these investment vehicles are not the same as the disclosure document regardless of whether the disclosure document is an offering memorandum, prospectus or offering circular.

What is the underlying plan? Many filmmakers and others who sit down to write a business plan experience writer's block or are otherwise intellectually paralyzed because they have failed to organize their thinking and make the necessary preliminary decisions relating to their proposed business venture. These early questions form the basis of the underlying plan that is described in the business plan. If the questions have not been considered and decisions made, it is extremely difficult to write about nonanswers or be consistent in writing about those decisions throughout the document. In other words, before writing a business plan, which is the documentation of the actual underlying plan, a filmmaker first must have an underlying plan. There must be some well-thought-out ideas behind the physical representation of the plan ordinarily referred to as a business plan.

So, let's first examine some questions that any filmmaker starting out to write a business plan needs to ask. For example, this actual plan must include consideration of choice of entities and investment vehicles, along with the deal between the filmmaker and the investor. To come up with this basic plan, the following questions need to be answered:

Is the filmmaker seeking to raise money from investors for purposes of funding a particular phase in the life of a film company or to finance the costs associated with a specific film project?

Is the filmmaker seeking to raise some start-up funds at the company's start-up phase or seeking to raise money for a particular project or project phase?

What form of doing business or entity should the filmmaker choose for the development, production or distribution company?

Is that the same entity that will be used to raise some or all of the funds sought from investors (i.e., does the filmmaker want investors to own a piece of the company or a profit participation in the revenue stream of one or more specific projects)?

Will an investment vehicle that is separate from the production company be used to raise funds from investors?

Is the filmmaker planning to raise money from active or passive investors? In other words, is the filmmaker willing to allow investors to be regularly involved in helping make the important decisions that will need to be made (active investors)? Or does the filmmaker want the investors to be passive, thus reserving the management rights to the filmmaker and his or her associates?

Once revenues generated by the exploitation of the film flow back to the production entity, what is the revenue-sharing ratio between the production entity and the investor or investors?

Are the investors allowed some form of priority recoupment? That is, does the percentage of revenues that flow to the investors start out high and then become smaller after their originally invested capital is repaid,

plus some form of bonus, before the revenue-sharing split settles into
its final ratio?

Is the filmmaker seeking financing for a single film project or multiple
film projects?

What film genre best describes the film, and what is its anticipated MPAA
rating?

Is the filmmaker looking to the business plan's active investors to provide
100 percent of the financing needed or some other percentage?

Possible alternative underlying plans for film-related business plans that may be
useful to filmmakers include:

Development of single motion picture. Use a sole proprietorship as the
production/development company (with a fictitious name or dba) and
one or more investor-financing agreements to raise development funds
for a single motion picture from several active investors.

Slate development. Use a regular C corporation or an S corp to raise money
from a small group of founding shareholders in a corporation to be
formed upon successfully raising the money sought through the business plan; use the corporate funds to develop a slate of family-oriented
(G- and PG-rated) motion pictures for distribution through DVD sales
exclusively.

Coproduction. Use a production company to join with another company
through a joint-venture agreement (coproduction deal) for which the
filmmaker's company provides the script and some of the production
financing, and the other company provides the balance of the financing
along with some talent for the purpose of producing a single action/
adventure film (or other genre) for theatrical release.

Completion fund. Use the member-managed LLC (development/production
company) to raise money from four or five additional member-managers
for the purpose of creating a completion fund to help other low-budget
independent filmmakers complete their films that are almost finished
but stalled at the lab due to lack of funds.

Equity component. Using one of the active-investor investment vehicles in
combination with a business plan to raise a portion of a film's production budget, the balance of which is sought through various forms of
lender financing (negative pickups, foreign presales, and the like) and
cash-flowing tax incentives.

Business-plan consultants and others sometimes take a position that an investor-financed development deal is more risky for the investors than a production
deal. But there is no statistical support for such a position. It really depends on

the project, how much money is being raised, the producer's plan for production financing, the producer's relationships with potential production-financing sources and other factors. So, making a statement to the effect that providing money for development is always a greater risk than providing money for production financing is merely someone's opinion and not supported by the facts.

With respect to investor-financed development deals, however, filmmakers and their prospective investors often want to know how the investors are supposed to get their money back and, it is hoped, make a profit. Film-development deals offer several options for investor recoupment and profit taking: First, the investors may be paid back their early investment in the development of a project out of the film's subsequently determined production budget. It is not uncommon in the film industry for a major studio that develops a film project but decides not to go forward with the production to sell that project to another studio or production entity. In such cases, the developing entity will certainly want to recoup its investment and possibly make a profit on its development activities. The same is true for an investor-financed film project. Assuming there is a willing buyer, the film project has been developed effectively and the investor money has not been squandered, there is no reason why the group that put up the money to develop a project could not recoup and expect to make a profit off their development activities. It is true that development of film projects is a very competitive environment, but so is the production of films, as well as distribution. It's all competitive. Secondly, a development group of investors may negotiate with the development executive/producer to participate in the salary to be paid to such individual out of the film's production budget if this individual also works on the production of the film in some capacity. After all, the investor funds made it possible for the film project to move beyond development to make it ready for production financing. Finally, the development investors may also be allowed to participate in a distributor advance (if any), the producer's share of the film's net profits or other defined stages in the film's revenue stream.

Development executives, producers and investors have to be careful, however, when negotiating for a profit participation expressed as "points." This term is one of those words of art that traditionally refers to a profit participation at a specific point in a film's revenue stream, that is, in a film's "net profits." Expressing the profit participation as a percentage of a film's net profits also means 100 percent of the film's net profits. In other words, if the profit participation is 5 percent of the film's net profits, the percentage itself automatically means 5 parts of 100 parts. On the other hand, many long-time entertainment-industry practitioners, specifically entertainment attorneys and agents, insist that this profit participation be expressed as 5 percent of 100 percent of the film's net profits, which is redundant. Nevertheless, they will generally insist that the participation be written that way. The presumed reason, of course, is that it is not uncommon for a film's production entity to receive less than 100 percent of a film's net profits. In fact, there is little to no authoritative information available regarding the average or typical net-profit split between the distributor and production company on independent films. Another reason why such persons insist on the redundancy is that they often just say "net profit" and fail to make clear that the percentage participation applies to the "film's net profits" as opposed to, for example, the production company's net profits. This confusion also suggests that the term "net profits" should never be used to describe two different places in a film's revenue stream.

In any case, after a distributor takes out its distribution fee and then recoups its distribution expense (in the traditional acquisition distribution deal), the distribution agreement will typically state what percentage of the film's net profits will flow to any profit participants who have negotiated a profit participation. If that net-profit participation for the production company is 50 percent of the film's net profits, but the production company agreed to pay some other profit participant 5 percent of the film's net profits (i.e., 5 points), the production company will only have 50 percent of the film's net profits out of which it is obligated to pay 5 percent of the film's net profits. Thus, the production company will have to calculate what percentage of 50 percent of the film's net profits is the same as 5% of the film's net profits, precisely because the production company does not control (i.e., will never be paid) 100 percent of the film's net profits—that was not the bargain. In this instance, the calculation is fairly easy. Ten percent of the production company's share is equal to 5 percent of the film's net profits. But, if the percentage of the production company's participation is more or less than 50 percent, the calculation becomes more difficult.

For these reasons, it may make more sense for an investor-financed development group partly relying on a profit participation in the film's revenue stream to simply express that participation as a percentage of the producer's share (assuming for purposes of this discussion that the producer is the same individual or entity that served as the development executive on the investor-financed development deal) and not as "points" or even as a percentage of the film's net profits. This profit-participation deal between the development investors and the producer is being negotiated before the negotiation of the deal between the producer and the distributor. So, the producer has no idea what percentage of the film's net profits may be granted to the production company by the distributor in their subsequent negotiations.[9]

The filmmaker's underlying plan may also include consideration of the various federal, state or international tax incentives relating to film development, production or distribution. Another strategy may involve raising a limited amount of money from investors for the purpose of developing one or more film projects and then seeking one or more production loans with which to produce the film(s) (e.g., worldwide negative pickup, split-rights deal, foreign presales, gap financing and so forth).

These preliminary considerations need to be determined by the filmmaker and his or her team in advance and kept firmly in mind during the entire process of drafting the business plan. Otherwise, language that is inconsistent with this underlying plan will inevitably creep into the document, and some prospective investors may notice it, be distracted by it or, even worse, assume that the filmmaker does not know what he or she is talking about.

Deferring decisions and negotiating later. Some business-plan consultants actually recommend that holding off making certain of these important preliminary decisions, specifically relating to the investment vehicle, until the filmmaker has some interested investors and that the filmmaker then negotiate with the investors themselves to determine which investment vehicle would best serve their and the filmmaker's needs. That is an option. However, this book, in providing guidance to filmmakers during this process of raising money with a business plan, endeavors to give the filmmaker an understanding of what the options are in investment vehicles in order to go into negotiations prepared. If the filmmaker does not know the differences, advantages and disadvantages among the various investment vehicles available with a business plan seeking a few active investors, he or she is at a decided disadvantage when negotiating with those investors. As a consequence, the investors are more likely to lower their regard for the filmmaker's business sense, and such negotiations are less likely to be successful for the filmmaker. Or even worse, it would be reasonable for a prospective investor to conclude that the filmmaker's plan is not complete without the choice of investment vehicle and without the actual deal between the investor and the filmmaker. Those are two very important issues that are likely to come up when asking anyone to consider investing money.

Here again is another set of preliminary decisions that the filmmaker must make:

Should I do the research in advance but hold off on deciding which investment vehicle is best suited for my particular purpose and thus not disclose in the business plan what that choice is?

Should I do the research in advance and decide which investment vehicle is best suited for my particular purposes and include that information in the business plan, along with a copy of the proposed agreement or other relevant documentation (as one or more exhibits)?

Should I ignore this subject altogether and scramble around at the last minute when an investor gets serious and negotiate blindly with the investor about the most suitable investment vehicle (and the deal between us) knowing that the prospective investor may or may not be any more sophisticated about such things than I am?

The last choice is the worst possibility, but that is actually the approach recommended by some business-plan consultants because they make no effort to include considerations relating to the various available forms of active-investor investment vehicles in their articles or books on the subject. As noted above, some business-plan consultants recommend the first choice, but the downside is that the investors will not be impressed or that the filmmaker will lose the investment because of snags in the subsequent negotiations. The middle choice appears more reasonable because the filmmaker demonstrates that he or she has studied the matter (i.e., choice of investment vehicle), is familiar with the various available forms of active-investor investment vehicles and has made an informed choice for purposes of this specific investment. That should impress most prospective investors. Furthermore, if a prospective investor who seems to be interested in investing a significant amount of money into the film project takes the position that he or she would prefer a different investment vehicle, the filmmaker is free to open negotiations on the point and could choose to modify his or her initial choice.

Another approach would be to not commit in advance to a particular investment vehicle but to include a comprehensive discussion in the business plan describing the four most-likely investment vehicles that can be used with a business plan seeking funding from one or a few active investors. This approach allows a filmmaker to provide a framework for the discussions with investors.[10] This approach is more difficult to write about in a business plan.

Effect on financial projections. There are other practical problems with not specifying which investment vehicle is to be used and not ever disclosing information in the business plan relating to the revenue-sharing arrangement between the producer/management team and the investor or investor group. The problem is that the financial projections associated with such a business plan cannot take the future possible results of an investment all the way to the purchase of a single interest, unit or share of whichever investment vehicle is chosen. That's why sometimes when even the more sophisticated preparers of financial projections for film projects submit their financial projections, they tend to stop at the producer level and not proceed to the investor level, which is really what is of most interest to investors. The investors do not want to have to do their own calculations figuring in the revenue-sharing deal between the producer/management team and the investor(s) after the producer has merely provided the investor(s) with an estimate of the revenues that may become available to the producer. The investor, in most instances, would prefer that such calculations be done by the producer for the benefit of the investor (see chapter 10).

Another very practical problem with not choosing an investment vehicle in advance and including a discussion of that investment vehicle in the business plan is that without a specific investment vehicle, there is nothing for the investor who is ready to invest to sign. If a filmmaker takes the advice of some business-plan consultants and leaves out any discussion of the investment vehicle, when a prospective investor looks at the business plan and says, "Wow, that's a terrific idea for a movie. I'd like to be a part of that! Where do I sign?" the filmmaker would have to say, "Well first we need to talk about your preferences for an investment vehicle and negotiate the revenue-sharing arrangement as between us." That's a good way to lose that investor. It would seem more businesslike and preferable to present the prospective investor with a complete and fair proposal, not only including a business plan but also a specific investment vehicle, a stated revenue-sharing scheme, the complete financial projections and something for the investor to sign.

If the investment vehicle is the investor-financing agreement, the investor would sign that agreement itself. If the investment vehicle is the joint venture, the investor would sign the joint-venture agreement. If the investment vehicle is the corporation to be formed upon funding, the investor may be asked to sign a subscription agreement and then will ultimately be asked to sign the initial share-holder and board of directors minutes. If the investment vehicle is a member-managed LLC, the investor may be asked to sign an LLC operating agreement. So again, it is certainly more efficient to do the research, make these decisions ahead of time and present the prospective investor with a complete package that allows him or her to sign on the dotted line at the time of the presentation.

Once more, the useful investment vehicles for filmmakers using business plans include the following:

- investor financing agreement, which may state the revenue-sharing ratio as between the producer/management team and the investor(s);
- a joint venture agreement (domestic coproduction), which also may state the revenue-sharing deal;
- a corporation to be formed (either a regular C corporation or an S corp), which limits the revenues to be paid to investor/shareholders to dividends determined strictly in accordance with the percentage ownership of certain classes of stock; or
- a member-managed LLC which may provide a bit more flexibility in structuring the revenue-sharing deal in accordance with the LLC's operating agreement.

Company or project financing. Another important distinction that filmmakers need to clearly understand before starting to draft a business plan is the difference between company financing and project financing. With company financing, the filmmaker is seeking general financing for the long-term, ongoing activities of the company. The investors participate in the profits of the company in general and tend to be investors of the company for a long period of time. Usually, company financing is associated with the corporate investment vehicle but also may be associated with the use of the member-managed LLC. On the active-investor (nonsecurities) side, company financing may be undertaken by a corporation to be formed (the initial incorporation strategy); on the passive-investor side, company financing may be undertaken by selling shares in an existing corporation (i.e., a securities offering for which a business plan is not the appropriate informational document).

Project financing is raising the money for financing the costs associated with one or more limited-term projects. The investors are profit participants for a stated term in the revenue streams generated by the exploitation of the project (the film or films) but not the company generally. With active-investor investment vehicles, project financing is typically associated with the investor-financing agreement, the joint-venture agreement or the member-managed LLC. The passive-investor investment vehicles associated with project financing most commonly include the manager-managed LLC or the limited partnership. These latter two investment vehicles, as noted earlier, involve the sale of a security (i.e., a unit in the manager-managed LLC or a unit in the limited partnership), and, thus, use of a business plan is not appropriate. Instead, such offerings require the use of a securities disclosure document to communicate information to prospective investors. Thus, filmmakers must make an informed choice about which investment vehicle is most suited to the particular business venture being considered.

This brings up another point with respect to these preliminary choices and the language used in the business plan to reflect those choices. One of the common phrases used by business-plan preparers is "the company." That is appropriate if the filmmaker has chosen the company financing discussed above and the investment vehicle has been defined as "the company." In other words, if the filmmaker has chosen to use either the initial incorporation or member-managed LLC, only one company is typically involved, and it is the same as the investment vehicle. But, if a filmmaker chooses to use the investor-financing agreement or the joint-venture agreement as the investment vehicle and one of the parties to that contract is the filmmaker's production company or development company, that company is not the same as the investment vehicle, and the investors are not investing in the filmmaker's company. Under those circumstances, it makes little sense and is fairly confusing to constantly refer in the business plan to "the company."

However, when the filmmaker crosses that very important line between active investors and passive investors, not only does a filmmaker sometimes forget that the business plan is not the appropriate document for providing information to the investors but the filmmaker also gets confused about the arrangement typically involving a production company, for example, which may be serving as the general partner of a limited partnership or a manager of a manager-managed LLC. Thus, two companies or entities may be involved, and it needs to be made clear which entity is which instead of using the ambiguous phrase "the company." It is more appropriate to refer to the "general partner" of the limited partnership or the "manager" of the manager-managed LLC. These issues are only raised in the context of securities offerings because the limited partnership and the manager-managed LLC involve the sale of a security. Business-plan preparers should not have to deal with this specific issue except in cases where they are unaware that the filmmaker is seeking to raise money through the sale of a security, and both have failed to realize that the business plan is not the appropriate document to use. In this sense, the two-entity, passive-investor approach may serve as a red flag for both business-plan consultants and filmmakers.

Use of proceeds. Another important aspect of this basic, underlying plan is to determine how the investor funds are to be used. Some alternative plans regarding use of investor funds include:

- start up a new production/development company that will engage in the development and production of documentary films, feature films for theatrical release, feature films for release to DVD or a series of videos
- develop a single feature- or documentary-film project for theatrical release
- develop a slate of feature- or documentary-film projects for release in all markets and media
- produce a single feature film or documentary film for release in all markets and media
- produce a slate of feature films or documentary films for DVD release
- provide the equity component of the production costs for a film being financed through several funding sources
- create a completion fund to help other independent producers complete their feature- or documentary-film projects
- pay for some or all of an already produced film's distribution expenses through a rent-a-distributor deal or some form of self-distribution
- start up a feature-film- or DVD-distribution company

A Business Plan as Supplementary Material

When a filmmaker clearly knows he or she needs a securities disclosure document to provide information to prospective investors, because these filmmakers understand they are seeking to raise money from a group of passive investors and they are clearly selling a security (i.e., units in a limited partnership or manager-managed LLC or shares in an existing corporation), some business-plan consultants still advocate using a business plan as a supplement to the securities disclosure document. The underlying thinking (other than the self-serving motives) appears to be that a securities disclosure document has a lot of required information that is very legalistic or technical and thus is not an effective selling document. There has always been some tension between the dual nature of a securities disclosure document, just as there is with a business plan. This tension arises between the desire to sell the deal in the most positive terms and the need to comply with whatever legal requirements exist for such a document (i.e., compliance document versus selling document). It is true that many more requirements are imposed on the drafting of a securities disclosure document, but a business plan is not without restrictions itself.

The problem with the thinking that it is good to use a business plan to supplement a PPM is that if a business plan is used with a securities disclosure document to raise money from passive investors, the business plan becomes part of the securities offering, and the securities-compliance requirements apply just as much to the business plan as to the securities disclosure document. Thus, if a business plan intended to be used as supplementary material for a securities offering is not thoroughly reviewed and brought into compliance by the securities attorney who prepares the securities disclosure document, information in the business plan could create compliance problems for the filmmaker seeking to raise funds. Further, some of the information required in a securities disclosure document for a film offering is the same kind of information that is ordinarily seen in a business plan (e.g., narrative biographies, film-industry information, synopsis of the script, how investor money will be used, box-office comparables, and the like). Thus, by using a business plan as a supplement to a securities disclosure document, the filmmaker creates a high level of redundancy between the two documents and adds an unnecessary reading burden for the prospective investor, as well as more work for the securities attorney. Practically speaking, such an approach also adds expense to the process by causing the filmmaker to increase his or her drafting, copying and binding expenses.

The preferred solution is to use a business plan in those limited circumstances in which it is appropriate (that is, seeking money from one to a few active investors), but use a securities disclosure document when seeking money from a group of passive investors, and not both under any circumstances. In addition, more effort should be made by the filmmaker and the securities attorney in drafting a securities disclosure document to make it a more effective selling document. That eliminates what appears to be the primary underlying argument for use of a business plan as supplemental material for a securities disclosure document and avoids the risks and inefficiency associated with the duplication. In the alternative, supplement the PPM with a marketing brochure but not a full business plan. And use the copy already approved by the securities attorney in the PPM's offering summary as the text of the marketing brochure.

Business Plans and Fraud

Although the SEC's antifraud rule does not specifically apply to business plans, the common law concept of fraud, along with state and other federal statutory definitions of fraud, does apply. Thus, statements made in a business plan may lead to charges of fraud. Generally speaking, fraud is an intentional deception resulting in an injury to another. Fraud may be both a crime and a civil wrong. However, many elements make up fraud, so it may be difficult to prove in a court of law. That does not mean it is wise to draft the business plan in a shoddy, borderline or risky manner, using language that comes close to or crosses the line, thereby either encouraging or inviting a disgruntled investor to make a demand to return his or her invested funds or in the alternative to take the filmmaker to court.

The elements of fraud include a false and material misrepresentation is made by one who either knows it is false or is ignorant of its falsehood, the statement is made with the intent that the representation be relied on by the recipient (in a reasonable manner), the recipient does not know the representation is false and rightfully or justifiably relies on the representation, which in turn causes proximate injury to the recipient. Again, statements made in business plans may constitute fraud. If a filmmaker makes a false statement in a business plan and knows it is a false statement, the statement is made with the intent that the prospective investor rely on it, the prospective investor does not know the statement is false, the prospective investor relies on the statement (i.e., invests his or her money) and that reliance causes the loss of the investor's invested funds, the filmmaker may well be in court defending the statement. Thus, in writing a business plan, every statement needs to be objectively examined to determine whether it is a statement that is both true and can be defended in court. To use any other standard in drafting a business plan that is seeking money from investors is quite reckless.

Contingent promissory notes. The same is true for the contingent promissory note that some entertainment attorneys are fond of recommending to unsuspecting independent producers. Some attorneys sometimes suggest to filmmakers that instead of going to the trouble of selling a security through a passive-investor investment vehicle, just sell contingent promissory notes, with or without a business plan, and that will work. Unfortunately, this is bad advice, since the repayment of the promissory note (a loan) is made contingent on the film making money and returning money to the producer (that's what "contingent" means in such transactions). In such cases, the purported lenders have actually signed on to a profit-participation scheme, which is clearly a security.[11] Thus, these filmmakers are being advised by people who should know better to go out and commit the felony of selling an unregistered security, which, in turn, gives these purported lenders who are actually investors, the right to demand the return of their money since that is one of the civil remedies the securities laws provide (i.e., rescission of the contract and repayment of the invested funds). Of course, that could be a bit awkward after the money has been spent on producing the motion picture and could even lead to a malpractice lawsuit against the entertainment attorney who originally gave the bad advice.

It is important that these preliminary decisions regarding the basics of a plan be made prior to starting to draft the document referred to as the business plan, since these preliminary decisions regarding the actual or underlying plan have an impact on how a business plan is written. After all, if selling shares in a corporation to be formed upon funding, a filmmaker would want to be consistent throughout the document that he or she is selling shares, as opposed to, for example, selling units in a member-managed LLC. If the filmmaker mixes the terminology, prospective investors are likely to be confused and are less likely to favorably consider investing. Further, if the filmmaker is funding a start-up production/development company (company financing) as opposed to seeking financing for a single feature film (project financing), that will impact the information disclosed regarding use of proceeds (i.e., how the filmmaker expects to spend the money invested) and will also impact the preparation of the financial projections. So, these preliminary decisions have to be made, and they have to be based on solid reasoning that fits the particular company or project's needs.

If a filmmaker puts off decisions until after drafting the business plan begins, that increases the chances that he or she will become confused in the middle of writing the business plan or that some of the language in one part of the business plan will not be consistent with another portion of the same business plan. That is a very common occurrence when a filmmaker uses someone else's business plan as a template without carefully thinking through his or her own situation and underlying plan.

2. Cover Page and Table of Contents

What are the essentials that must be on the cover of a business plan, and who has the authority to make such rules? The answer to both questions is that there are no requirements relating to what must be on the cover of a business plan, because there is no authority that either makes or enforces such rules. This is one of the many differences between a business plan and a securities disclosure document. Both the federal and state governments have agencies that provide and enforce disclosure requirements relating to securities disclosure documents, including the information that must appear on the cover page. But no such agencies regulate the contents of a business plan, so common sense and custom prevail.

Cover

Most business-plan preparers would probably take the position that the cover of a business plan should at least say "Business Plan" in large, bold letters. It may also include a brief description of the purpose of the business plan (e.g., seeking to fund the production costs of a single feature-length motion picture). It could also include the amount of money being sought. In addition, a filmmaker may want to set out the name of the company or the name of the project on the cover page, possibly accompanied by some indication as to the nature of the investment vehicle. For example, if the investment vehicle is a corporation to be formed, the name on the cover page of the business plan may be "XYZ Film Productions Inc. (a California corporation to be formed)," or whatever other state in which the corporation may be formed. If the investment vehicle is a member-managed LLC, the name on the cover page may be "XYZ Film Productions LLC." The cover page may also include the company address and phone number and the date on which the business plan was first made available to prospective investors.

Some business-plan consultants recommend creating a space on the cover (e.g., upper-right-hand corner) to insert the name of the person receiving the business plan and a tracking number and keeping a list to track how many business plans were sent out and to whom. This is most likely another carryover from securities private-placement offering practices for which issuers are advised to keep track of their distribution of their securities disclosure documents as a means of creating evidence that a prohibited general solicitation did not occur. Although a good idea, this carryover is not required for business-plan distribution.

Picking and choosing from the cover-page requirements for a securities disclosure document, a business plan preparer might include the following:

name of the company or investment vehicle
the title, amount and description of the investment being offered
any current owners who are selling some of their interests (this needs to
    be disclosed)
a cross-reference to the risk-factors section if one exists
the date of the document

Although a risk-factors section is not required for a business plan, including one may be a good idea, just so investors do not later complain that the filmmaker did not tell them about some of the bad things that could happen to their investment (i.e., the risks associated with the investment—see "Risk Factors" section, chapter 11).

Since a film is not only a business venture but also a creative enterprise, filmmakers may also want to include some sort of artwork on the front cover of a business plan. If art is already created for a one-sheet, sell-sheet or poster relating to a feature film or documentary, this same artwork may be available for the business plan's cover. Otherwise, some form of art or graphic design will tend to enhance the cover and help communicate that this business plan is for a creative venture as opposed to less-artistic business enterprises. A sample cover page, without spacing, bold or font changes, follows.

Business Plan
Providing information for the purpose of raising
$1,000,000 (minimum) to $2,000,000 (maximum)
from one to three active investors
and members of a member-managed LLC
to be formed upon funding
in units of $500,000 each
for use in producing a single motion picture
for exploitation in all markets and media
throughout the world.
XYZ Film Productions
1234 Avenue F

Los Angeles, California 91362

(310) 583–3429

September 15, 2010

Table of Contents

A table of contents, sometimes referred to only as "Contents," is a listing of the parts of a business plan (or other lengthy written document), accompanied by the page numbers where the parts listed appear in the document. It is organized in the order the topics are presented, and its purpose is to offer the reader a quick overview of the contents of the business plan and where to find each item. The index also provides a way for readers to find specific information, but an index is organized alphabetically and is not typically associated with a business plan.

The table of contents generally includes the major headings (i.e., the most important sections) of the business plan, and often subheadings are included. Although some business-plan consultants claim that the major headings for a business plan are fairly standard, a quick review of a sample of books on writing business plans shows that no such standards exist, particularly when working on a film-related business plan. Some major headings will change depending on whether the business plan is being written for planning purposes or for seeking lender or investor financing or financing for a company or a project. The major headings may also change depending on the investment vehicle being used with the business plan. Such headings will also most certainly differ depending on the industry.

The depth of detail in the table of contents is pretty much a judgment call. Factors to consider are the length of the business plan, the number of major headings, the number of subheadings and the length of the table of contents when it is completed. From the reader's point of view, the table of contents is preferably no more than one page in length. That way, the reader can gain a quick understanding of how the business plan is organized. The more pages the table of contents runs, the more difficult it is for a reader to find his or her way around the overall document. The one-page table of contents also helps the business plan preparer as he or she works to put together the document because it is easier to visualize how the business plan is organized and how the parts relate to each other. Experimenting with margins, line spacing and font size offers some flexibility when trying to fit specific content into a single page.

In a business plan, the table of contents is usually located just behind the cover page. In the event that the business plan is copyrighted, the copyright notice may appear between the cover page and the table of contents. The table of contents would typically be followed in the business plan by the executive summary or business plan summary as some name that section.

When numbering pages, all pages are counted, including the cover page, although sometimes the table of contents commonly has a lowercase Roman numeral, and the summary (whether called an executive summary or business-plan summary) starts with page 1.

Examples of Tables of Contents

EXAMPLE 1

This table of contents is specifically for the production of a slate of low-budget, independently produced motion pictures and for use in seeking grant funds as opposed to investor financing. Subheadings are added. Some of the main headings use different titles than those suggested by the main chapter titles in this book.

EXAMPLE 2

This business plan example is for the production of a single, independently produced feature-film project. The reference in the financial projections section is merely a discussion of the purpose of the financial projections and refers the reader to the exhibit where the actual financial projections appear. This example lists more exhibits than example 1.

The headings of the sections and subsections above are discussed further in the following chapters.

It is useful to start preparation of a business plan by beginning with a draft table of contents. The draft gives a sense of the document's overall organization and helps determine where specific blocks of information most appropriately appear. As ideas occur to the filmmaker about the location of major sections relative to other sections, changes are made both in the body of the business plan and in the table of contents. Remember to also reflect changes in headings in major sections and subsections in the table of contents. Near the end of the first draft stage of the business plan itself, in the table of contents the filmmaker should add the leaders (. . .) (if used) between the headings and the page numbers, and insert page numbers that correspond with the location of the beginning of each listed section or subsection. Recognizing that those page numbers may change with further drafts, the last task to do after the filmmaker is satisfied with the business plan is to review the page numbers listed in the table of contents to confirm that they are consistent with the pages on which each listed section heading and/or subheading appears.

3. Executive Summary

In the context of a business plan being prepared for a film or film slate, this section may be called the "Business Plan Summary." After all, it may or may not be prepared for or read by executives. Thus, again, the "executive summary" language appears to be a carryover from business plans drafted for corporate funding. Executives are closely associated with corporations. Other business-plan preparers also suggest the alternative title of "Statement of Purpose" as either a substitute for the entire section or as a subsection heading within the business-plan summary.

This section is a summary of the business plan and focuses just on the main points. It may be thought of as a thesis statement. It leaves out the detail but sets out the objectives of the business, explains briefly who is involved (management or people section), may discuss some of the strengths of the planned venture, provides a quick analysis of why management believes the venture will succeed, explains the reason or reasons why investor financing is needed, what it will be used for, how much money is needed and how an investor may benefit from an investment.

Some business-plan consultants suggest that a summary ought to be limited to a specific number of sections (e.g., five sections), but it really should be organized in a manner that is similar to the organization of the overall business plan while providing an adequate summary of the plan. If that takes six or seven sections, so be it. Some business plans may require more summary subsections than others.

The most commonly recommended length for the business-plan summary appears to be two pages or so. Some business-plan preparers also include an unbound, one-page "summary of the summary" or a "highlights page," using a bulleted format to send out to prospective investors with an initial inquiry letter (i.e., the highlights page is not bound with the rest of the business plan).

The summary of a business plan ought to be formatted differently, that is, set apart from the main body of the business plan. A way to do that is to create headlines for each section of the summary and indent the accompanying text for each headline so that the headlines and the text are more visually separated. Readers can more easily search for the material that is of most interest to them. Underlining and bolding the headlines make them stand out from the rest of the text.

Most business-plan consultants also advise that the summary be prepared last. There is nothing wrong with that advice. It is perfectly logical to first draft the main body of the document, then come back and prepare the summary that will appear in the first few pages. But, if that does not work for the filmmaker, he or she should do it his or her way. After all, there is also nothing wrong with taking a stab at the summary, then expanding on each section of the summary to create the body of the business plan. In all likelihood, the preparer of a business plan is going to move back and forth between the two to keep these sections of the business plan consistent. In other words, it is not likely that the filmmaker will only make one pass at the summary, so what difference does it make whether he or she starts the first draft of the summary last or first? None at all. The filmmaker will be revisiting the summary from time to time anyway. So, if it is more comfortable starting with the summary because it helps organize thinking, by all means disregard the chorus of naysayers. Just be sure to come back to it several times and recheck for consistency as the rest of the business plan is constructed and changes.

One way to approach the writing of the business-plan summary is to simply draft a brief but factual story about the proposed business venture, without going into detail on any particular topic. Then break out each identifiable subtopic within the story, and recheck the ordering of the thoughts to make sure they seem to logically relate to each other. Then develop each of those thoughts or subtopics into a paragraph, and give it an appropriate subheading. Add enough information for each subsection to create at least a three- or four-sentence paragraph but without covering all of the detail expected in the main body or major sections of the business plan. Then, finish each summary paragraph with a parenthetical reference to the more detailed version of that information found in the main body of the business plan.

Drafting tips

Go back over the series of paragraphs, and watch for and try to eliminate the exaggeration, flowery language, fluff, hyperbole, puffery and speculation so commonplace among filmmakers. Do not make the document overly promotional. Be as factual as possible. Investors will be more impressed with that. They are likely to see through the smokescreens. Also avoid making promises that cannot or may not be kept. In other words, avoid using words like "will" or "shall" when it may be more appropriate to say "may," "plans," "intends to," "anticipates," "hopes to" or "expects." Along the same lines, instead of making a flat-out statement that may or may not be able to be demonstrated as true, change the language so that it is a statement about the beliefs of the filmmaker (i.e., the filmmaker believes such and such). In other words, tone it down. That tends to soften the language and eliminates opportunities for the disgruntled investor to complain that something did not turn out the way it was promised (see discussion of fraud in chapter 1). Keep in mind that business plans are not strictly public relations (PR) documents. They must sell with facts not fluff. If the facts are not persuasive, strengthen them. Do not try to finesse the facts by writing around them.

Sample Executive-Summary Subheadings

As noted earlier, the outline of the executive summary should resemble the overall outline of the business plan itself. However, filmmakers tend to have a creative bent, so let's not limit that creativity to just a few set subheading possibilities. With that in mind, a variety of alternative possibilities are listed here. Some are slightly duplicative, others overlap, while still others suggest somewhat different information. A book on business plans should not limit the choices to those commonly used by businesspeople outside the film industry. In some instances, those simply do not work for a film deal. As a general rule, something in the neighborhood of six or seven headings ought to be able to express the key points for a business plan associated with one or more film projects. In other words, do not use all of the suggested headings set out as examples below. Pick and choose those most suited to the specific venture.

Overview

This subheading provides a brief summary of the entire business plan, for example:

> This business plan, used in conjunction with the selected investment vehicle described herein, offers a few qualified investors the opportunity to participate in the production, distribution and profit potential of a single feature-length motion picture.

The Opportunity

This subheading (which could also be called "The Investment Opportunity") focuses more on the opportunity for the film company and for the investor or investors:

> The XYZ Film Production Company has acquired the rights to an action/ adventure script and offers investors the opportunity to participate in the financing of the production and distribution of a single feature-length motion picture for worldwide distribution in all markets and media.

Objectives

This subheading may also provide an overview or a statement of the opportunity but with a focus on certain specific objectives:

> By means of this Business Plan and the accompanying Investor Financing Agreement (see Exhibit A), XYX Film Production Company (the 'Production Company') intends to finance, produce and distribute a single feature-length Motion Picture that promotes the theme that people need to be civil towards one another, with an estimated production budget of approximately $1,850,000. In addition, the Production Company may engage in distribution activities for such Picture through a joint venture or otherwise, so as to:
>
> 1. provide a reasonable return on investment for one to three active Investors; and
> 2. minimize the downside risk to the active Investors by financing, producing and owning a Motion Picture in the low budget range.

Mission Statement

The "Mission Statement" is one of those traditional subheadings often seen in the business-plan summary. The concept of a mission statement is more closely associated with a company or corporate business plan, where there may be a need to express to prospective long-term investors ideas relating to the management's overall philosophy. Thus, a mission statement is the broadest expression of a venture's purpose for existing. It differs from the underlying plan described in chapter 1, in that the underlying plan is a more practical expression of management's sense of how it anticipates accomplishing its objectives. In a business plan being used for project financing (i.e., raising money for financing one or more phases of or one or more film projects), the mission statement is not as important and may be left out. In the alternative, something akin to a mission statement may be merged with the more practical underlying plan. A mission statement may include information about the moral/ethical orientation of the venture, how it wants to be viewed by the public, important strategic influences, the film's target audience, description of the film or films, the geographic area where the film may be distributed and anticipated profitability.

Examples may include:

- developing and producing family films for worldwide distribution that are entertaining while providing moral guidance
- producing ethical films featuring women in realistic and nonstereotypical roles
- distributing films that entertain and enlighten the world
- producing films using cutting-edge technology and special effects

Purpose of the Business Plan

The idea behind this possible subheading is to make it clear exactly how the business plan is being used.

> The use of this Business Plan is limited to the purpose of identifying one or several prospective active Investors (or an active joint-venture partner) and providing information to such prospective Investors relating to the proposed feature-length movie project, its management and the film industry generally. This business plan is not suitable for use in the solicitation of passive investors. NO SECURITIES ARE OFFERED HEREBY. The business plan is merely an informational document used for the purpose of involving one or more active investors in the production of the Film.

The Company

Use of this traditional subheading may be limited to situations in which investors are being asked to actually invest in a company. Otherwise, it may be misleading to use this phrase or subhead. In other words, if the company and the investment vehicle are the same, such as with the initial incorporation or the member-managed LLC, it would be appropriate to provide the name of that company, the type of company, who its current owners are or who the company's promoters are, the address of the company's office, its phone number, the purpose of the company and so forth.

> The XYZ Film Production Company is a feature-film development/production company based in Burbank, California. The Company is organized as a California member-managed LLC and is currently wholly owned by the individual filmmakers James Okra and Penelope Davenport. Its offices are located at 1313 Maryland Avenue, Burbank, California 91505; phone (213) 456-7290.

The Production Company

This subheading is similar to "The Company" but goes past the more generic heading to provide more specific information in the subheading itself (i.e., that the company is a production company). Otherwise, the information contained in the summary paragraph would be the same or similar to that provided under "The Company" heading.

Investment Vehicle

The "Investment Vehicle" subheading may differ from "The Company" heading in the sense that the two may not be the same. A filmmaker or filmmakers may have a company that is organized as a sole proprietorship (possibly operating under a fictitious name), a general partnership, a corporation or a member-managed LLC. On the other hand, the investment vehicle may be an investor financing agreement, a joint-venture agreement, a corporation to be formed or another member-managed LLC. These likely combinations are:

Production Company	*Investment Vehicle*
Sole proprietorship	Investor financing agreement
Sole proprietorship	Joint-venture agreement
General partnership	General partnership
General partnership	Joint-venture agreement
Existing corporation	Joint-venture agreement
Corporation to be formed	Corporation to be formed
Member-managed LLC	Member-managed LLC

For even more clarity, let's describe these same concepts and how they relate to the headings in a business-plan summary:

Sole proprietorship and investor financing agreement. If the production company is operating as a sole proprietorship, it may use the investor financing agreement or the joint-venture agreement as the investment vehicle. Thus, in those two situations, the company and the investment vehicle would be different, thereby requiring two different paragraphs in the summary, along with two different subheadings.

General partnership. If the production company is operating as a general partnership, it may be able to add investors as general partners (pursuant to the terms of the partnership agreement), and in that situation, the company and the investment vehicle would be the same. Thus, no separate paragraph or heading would be needed.

General partnership and joint venture. If the production company is operating as a general partnership and it chooses to use the joint-venture agreement as the investment vehicle, in that situation, the production company and the investment vehicle would be different (two paragraphs and two headings).

Existing corporation and joint venture. If the production company is already formed as a corporation (an existing corporation), it may seek to raise money through the use of a joint-venture agreement, and in that situation, the company and the investment vehicle would be different (two paragraphs and two headings). Note that the option of selling shares in an existing corporation is not included here because that involves the sale of a security, thus the business plan is not the appropriate document to use for providing information to investors. In that situation, a securities disclosure document would be required (see discussion in chapter 1).

Initial incorporation. If one or more individual filmmakers not currently operating as a film company decide to round up a few investors and form a new corporation, that corporation to be formed would be both the production company and the start-up investment vehicle, assuming the funds raised in forming this new corporation would be adequate to cover the costs of the anticipated business activity (only one paragraph and one heading in the summary).

Member-managed LLC. If one or more individual filmmakers not currently operating as a film company decide to round up a few investors and form a member-managed LLC, that member-managed LLC would be both the production company and the investment vehicle (one paragraph and one heading). In addition, since the member-managed LLC is an active-investor investment vehicle, one or more individual filmmakers could go ahead and form a member-managed LLC and then seek out a few more active investors to invest in their member-managed LLC, so long as the LLC's operating agreement allowed new investors to be brought in as members. In that situation, the company and the investment vehicle are still the same (one paragraph and one heading).

Organizational Plan

This broad subheading implies a discussion of how the company and even the investment vehicle are organized and how the investors relate to the company or both.

> The XYZ Film Development Group is organized as an Arizona member-managed LLC. The LLC's articles of organization were filed with the Arizona Secretary of State in February of 2008. The current owners of the company ("Original Member/Managers") are the individual filmmakers James P. Diddle and Wanda Ontune. The company's headquarters are located at 111 Dainwood Drive, Peoria, Arizona 85345; phone (623) 444-3435.

Management

This subheading implies that the subsequent paragraph(s) will contain some information about how the company or investment vehicle will be managed, along with some brief information about the backgrounds of those currently involved in management.

> The company (member-managed LLC) will be managed by all of its member-managers. The current or original member-managers include James P. Diddle, who will also serve as the Film's director. Mr. Diddle has directed three feature-length film projects to date. His associate, who is one of the original member-managers of the company, is Wanda Ontune, who has served as a line producer on more than ten independently produced feature films. (For more complete biographies of the key people associated with the project, see "People of XYZ Film Production Company").

The Management Team

This subheading is a bit more specific than "The Management" and focuses on the backgrounds of the people involved, as well as how they are involved. Note that an individual may be an owner of the company, may have another title in the company (e.g., president, vice-president, general partner, member-manager and the like) and also may have another title in the form of a screen credit. So, that an owner of the company (e.g., general partner, joint-venture partner, shareholder or member-manager) may also be the film's executive producer, producer, director, screenwriter, director of photography and so on.

> All important management decisions will be made by the LLC's member-managers acting together. The LLC's original member-manager, James P. Diddle, who has experience directing feature films, will serve as the director for the LLC's Film. Producing responsibilities will be managed by Wanda Ontune, who has served as a line producer on more than ten independently produced feature films. (For more complete biographies of the key people associated with the project, see "People of The XYZ Film Production Company.")

People of XYZ Films

This subheading is very similar in nature to the previous two but by implication recognizes that film projects often involve significant contributions from people who are neither owners nor management of the production company. For this reason, the headings "Management" or "The Management Team" may not work well for project financing for a feature film. A broader section heading is more on target. After all, filmmakers often bring in executive producers, producers, line producers, directors and others just to work on a single film project, and these individuals may not assume any management role in any affiliated company, nor become owners of such a company.

Management Compensation

This is not a subheading that needs to appear in the executive summary, but in the spirit of full disclosure, a filmmaker may choose to include such information to allay investor concerns about the filmmakers taking too much money out of the investor funds before the investors even recoup their investment. Such a tactic is often referred to as "front-end loading." (See further discussion of this topic in chapter 9.)

The Products

This subheading is another that may be a carryover from the more traditional and generic language of business plans and thus is not that useful for film-related business plans. Obviously, the product of a film-related business plan is the film or films, although it could be a DVD not intended for theatrical release. Since the phrase "The Products" is so generic, it is not really recommended for use with film-related business plans. Any of the following three alternative headings seem to be preferable.

The film or films. This subheading could also be called "Description of Movie Project." It provides basic information about the proposed film, including the film's tentative title, its genre, a brief description of the script's story, the setting for the film and where it may be produced (tentative locations), along with its anticipated Motion Picture Association of America (MPAA) rating.

> If funded as described above, the LLC intends to acquire the rights to the Script (i.e., the Screenplay entitled *Hope Is behind Us*), produce the feature film described herein and then arrange for the distribution of the Film. The Screenplay is a contemporary drama/comedy about a grown woman with the mind of a young girl who recruits her eccentric friends to help her find a stolen ancient artifact that contains the ashes of her deceased father (see "Description of Business—Script Synopsis"). The Picture is expected to receive an MPAA rating of PG or PG-13. Locations are set in Travis and Burnet Counties of Texas (see "Description of Business—Production Strategy" and "Estimated Use of Proceeds").

The film project. Use this subheading when drafting a business plan designed to raise funds for a film's development phase.

The market. As an alternative subheading for this traditional section, some may want to use "Market Overview/State of the Industry" to provide information including current statistics about the industry in which the business venture intends to compete. Information about the marketplace will likely be based on research regarding the film industry and should be supported with citations to sources. For independent films, the independent film sector ought to be discussed, along with the target audience for the film or films. A sentence or two in this summary section may be devoted to anticipated competition and an average box-office gross for similar films may also be included from the box-office comparables section in the main body of the business plan. Statistics, of course, need to be updated and current as possible.

> Market Overview/State of the Industry—Feature films continue to be a somewhat recession-resistant segment of the entertainment industry and the general economy with domestic box-office totals reaching $9.62 billion for 2007, the best year on record. The figure represents a 5 percent gain over 2006 and a 4 percent increase over the previous highest year of 2002. Admissions, however, were up only 1 percent over 2006 and were down when compared to 2002. The total number of films released in the United

States in 2007 remained on par with 2006 at 603 films. Domestic theatre admissions held steady at 1.4 billion tickets in 2007. [Source: www.mpaa. org] The independent sector remains very competitive. The Sundance Film Festival (held in Park City, Utah, late in January each year and often promoted as the foremost platform for American independent cinema) in 2008 received 3,624 feature-film submissions total (2,021 from the United States and 1,603 international films). These numbers represent an increase from last year when 1,852 U.S. and 1,435 international feature-length films were considered. Of those, 121 feature-length films were selected including 87 world premieres, 14 North American premieres and 12 U.S. premieres representing 25 countries and 55 first-time filmmakers. [Source: "Sundance Announces 2008 Lineup," *ShowBuzz*, www.showbuzz.cbsnews.com, November 29, 2007].

Marketing and Distribution

This subheading and paragraph deal with what happens to the film after it has been produced, and the marketing part relates more to how the producer will market the completed film to prospective distributors as opposed to the marketing a distributor will engage in on behalf of the film once a distribution deal is secured.

The Producers of *XYZ Film* will begin to seek distribution during preproduction since it is never too early to create "buzz" in the worldwide film communities. During production, the Producers plan to design a Web site and cut a trailer that can be sent to possible national and international distributors and other media companies to continue to garner interest. Among other things, the Producers will seek to enter *XYZ Film* in high-profile film festivals like Cannes, Sundance, Toronto, Venice and Berlin in order to generate positive word-of-mouth and critical "buzz."

Financial Matters

This subheading is very broad and may include all information that is financial in nature and may be of interest to prospective investors. That might cover historical financial information about the company or the investment vehicle, the prior performance of previous investment vehicles managed by the same company (if any), how management plans to use the investor funds (use of proceeds or estimated use of proceeds) and estimates as to the financial outcome of the investment looking into the future (financial projections).

Financial History

This subheading, recommended by some business-plan consultants, is more suited to companies that have been in business for a significant period of time and for which financial information actually exists. If that is the case, a film-maker may want to include in this section of the summary a brief overview of financial information about the company from the time it was first organized to the present. That might include some of the more traditional financial measures such as current assets, liabilities, cash flow, income and so forth. But, for most film projects being financed independently, it is entirely likely that a filmmaker will not be dealing with an established production company that can offer any of that sort of financial information. With that in mind, it might be more appropriate to avoid the use of "History" in this heading and opt instead for "Financial Plan," which is a bit more forward looking.

> The member-managed LLC is to be formed upon funding, thus no financial information is currently available. If funded as proposed in this business plan, investor funds will be used to acquire rights to the Script, produce the Film and seek distribution arrangements (see "Estimated Use of Proceeds").

Prior Performance

This possible subheading is somewhat similar to "Financial History" in that it implies there has been some history to report. It actually is a heading borrowed from securities disclosure documents when the producer/management group has been involved in raising money from investors in the past for other film projects. Thus, the idea is to disclose to prospective investors on the current project how those investments turned out.

Financial Highlights

This is a good subheading to use for the summary because it clearly implies that the filmmaker is just providing the most important financial information here.

Investment Matters

This subheading draws attention to the information that relates directly to the investment, the amount of money being sought from investors, the nature of the investment (i.e., profit participation through an investor financing agreement or a joint-venture agreement, shares in a corporation to be formed or units in a member-managed LLC), the share or unit price and limitations on the number of shares or units that may be purchased by any single investor, if any. This heading may also be called "Nature of Investment" (see that subhead in the sample below).

Investment Opportunity

This subheading is similar to the "Investment Matters" subheading although the word "opportunity" is a bit more positive than the word "matters."

Investor Profit Participation

If the investment is structured as a profit participation through an investor financing agreement or a joint-venture agreement, this might be the more appropriate subheading, since both of those investment vehicles offer a profit participation in the revenue stream of the film. Thus, this subheading is more specific than "Investment Opportunity."

Financial Projections

These are the hypothetical results of an investment in a film or film slate in the event that certain stated assumptions prove accurate. Financial projections are estimates (based on reasonable assumptions that should be disclosed) of the future financial results of an investment and the activities relating to the pro-duction, distribution and exploitation of a film or films. Only a summary of the calculations along with some of the key assumptions would be included here in the business-plan summary. Although financial projections are not required for a business plan (see discussion of financial projections in chapter 10), investors tend to want to see them, and they provide a useful point of discussion for film producers. Some of the most common questions asked by investors in film deals are "How do I get my money back?" and "How does the cash flow back to me?" It is important for the producer to understand that side of the transaction and be able to engage in an intelligent discussion regarding this subject. Actively participating in the preparation of the financial projections will help provide this understanding (see chapter 10).

Pro Forma Financial Statements

Some authors equate pro forma financial statements with financial projections, stating that pro forma financial statements are financial forms (invoices, profit-and-loss statements, balance sheets, and the like) based on future expectations. However, other definitions add a different wrinkle saying that pro forma financial statements are financial presentations that are designed to demonstrate the effect of a future or hypothetical transaction or event by showing how it might have affected the historical financial statements if it had been consummated during the period covered by those statements. Because of this apparent definitional confusion, it would appear more investor friendly to use the term "financial projections," which seems more clear on its face and leave the pro forma lan-guage to the accountants and MBAs who apparently like to use such vague or ambiguous terms.

Considering the above possibilities for subheadings and paragraphs within the business-plan summary or executive summary if preferred, it is clear that multiple titles are available for the five to seven subheadings and paragraphs traditionally seen. Each suggests a slightly different type of information for the paragraph or paragraphs to follow the subheading, thus film producers and business-plan preparers must sort through the available titles and attempt to choose those that most accurately describe the information being communicated to prospective investors. The filmmaker's job after making several passes at drafting the summary is to step back and, trying to be as objective as possible, determine whether he or she has included all of the main points relating to the proposed investment transaction and project. In other words, has the filmmaker briefly touched on all of the important points that the reasonable prospective investor would consider important as he or she considers an investment? If the filmmaker and his or her associates feel that this objective is met, they are very likely to have an adequate summary for the business plan.

Because this section is merely a summary of the business plan, each subsection should provide a reference to the main section of the business plan that offers details and support information for the topic addressed in that subsection.

Example of a Business-Plan Summary
Summary of the Business Plan

Objectives. By means of this Business Plan and the accompanying Investor Financing Agreement (see Exhibit *"A"*), *XYZ Entertainment Inc.* (the "Production Company") intends to finance, produce and distribute a single feature-length Motion Picture that promotes the theme that animals should be treated decently, with an estimated production budget of approximately $1,650,000. In addition, the Production Company may engage in distribution activities for such Picture through a joint venture or otherwise, so as to:

1. provide a reasonable return on investment for one to three active Investors; and
2. minimize the downside risk to the active Investors by financing, producing and owning a Motion Picture in the low-budget range.

Purpose of business plan. The use of this Business Plan is limited to the purpose of identifying one or several prospective active Investors (or an active joint-venture partner) and providing information to such prospective Investors relating to the proposed feature-length movie project, its management and the film industry generally. This business plan is not suitable for use in the solicitation of passive investors. NO SECURITIES ARE OFFERED HEREBY. The business plan is merely a vehicle used for the purpose of involving one or more active investors in the production of the Film.

The company. The production company responsible for all aspects of the project is XYZ Entertainment Inc., a California corporation and feature film production and development company with offices in Agoura Hills, California, a suburb of Los Angeles. The Company is wholly owned by the individual filmmaker Bobby Delay. The firm's Los Angeles area offices are located at 3211 Cameron Valley Road, Agoura Hills, California 95940; phone (818) 304-5962. Bobby Delay created the concept for the Movie project to be produced and will serve as one of the film's Producers (see biographical information at "XYZ Entertainment Inc.").

Management. The management of XYZ Entertainment Inc. will be primarily responsible for the management of the project, along with the Investor(s) who invest through the Investor Financing Agreement. Thus, the Investor(s) will be considered part of the project's management team. They will be supported in project management activities by appropriate staff and consultants (see "XYZ Entertainment Inc.").

Description of movie project. When the film's budget is fully funded, the Production Company intends to produce and arrange for distribution of a single feature-length motion picture based on a movie script to be selected because it promotes the theme that animals ought to be treated decently. The film's anticipated MPAA rating is PG-13 or G (see "Estimated Use of Proceeds").

Management compensation. Management of the Production Company will waive receipt of any compensation relating to the raising of any funds for the Project (i.e., in the nature of organization and management fees). Management has reserved its rights, however, to be reimbursed out of the funds raised through means of an Investor Financing Agreement, Joint Venture Agreement or other active-investor financing vehicle associated with this Business Plan for expenses incurred in connection with arranging for production-money financing and for development of the project. No consideration will be paid to the individual Bobby Delay for services in connection with the actual production of the Picture (see "Management and Affiliate Compensation").

Prior performance. Producer/Director/Actor Bobby Delay has limited experience managing production-financing offerings relating to film, but he is an experienced filmmaker. This project serves as his fourth opportunity to participate in the production of feature films as Producer. He has also produced multiple television documentaries. In addition, other experienced film-industry professionals will be added to the project as funding is achieved (see "XYZ Entertainment Inc. Management" and "Critical Reviews/One Sheets" in Exhibit B).

Investor percentage participation. As consideration for providing funding for the Picture, the Active Investor(s) or Joint-Venture Partner(s) will have an equity-ownership interest in the revenue stream generated by the exploitation of this movie project in all markets and media throughout the world. Such interest will entitle the Investor(s) to recoup 125 percent of his, her, their or its investment out of net revenues received by the Production Company for the exploitation of the Picture in all markets and media. After this defined level of Investor Recoupment has been achieved, a 50 percent percentage participation in all net revenues paid to the Production Company in relation to the exploitation of this Picture (in the form of distributor advances or percentage participations in a defined stage of the Film's revenue stream) will be paid to the Investor(s).

Nature of investment. The Active Investor(s) investment contemplated herein will not result in an equity investment in the Production Company itself. Such investment merely creates an equity interest (percentage participation) in the revenues generated by the exploitation of the Movie (the Picture) and paid to the Production Company for rights to distribute or otherwise exploit the completed Movie. This investment opportunity is limited to a few active investors, meaning they must be regularly involved in helping make the important decisions associated with the project, and to qualify as active investors, they must have knowledge of and experience in the film industry.

Investment term. The percentage participation interest of the Investor(s) shall terminate as of the end of ten (10) years from the start of principal photography on the Picture to be produced or at another earlier time specifically agreed to by the Investor(s) and the Producer.

Drafting Tips

Do not expect to be able to draft the business plan summary, any section of a business plan or the entire plan itself in one sitting. That is not a reasonable expectation. This means, of course, that when the filmmaker is not at the computer actually writing, he or she may well have a useful thought that would be good to insert at an appropriate place in the business-plan draft. A filmmaker should organize him- or herself so that he or she can document those random thoughts either by keeping an old-fashioned note pad handy or using a laptop or other technology to document thoughts. Then when the filmmaker gets back to the computer with some more writing time, he or she could go through those notes, expand on them and determine their placement in the overall document. By all means, do not lose those thoughts that occur away from the computer simply because there is no paper at hand to create a record of them. Once heavily involved in drafting such a document, the filmmaker's mind will inevitably continue to work on it even when the filmmaker is away from his or her desk or workspace.

4. The Company or Investment Vehicle

Once again, the more traditional major section of a business plan called "The Company" (or sometimes "Company Description") appears to be a carryover from the corporate business plans, in the sense that it is important in such business plans to spend some time talking about the company in which the investors are investing. In project financing, where investors may be investing in the revenue stream of one or more films but not investing in the production company, it may not be appropriate to name this section "The Company" and devote so much time and space to a discussion of the production or development company. Rather, it would be more appropriate to refer to the section as "The Investment Vehicle" and spend more time and space discussing the investment vehicle. For this reason, it is important to know the difference between the two and which applies to the filmmaker's specific situation.

Labeling the section "The Company" might be misleading or even confusing to prospective investors because by its very terms, this section heading implies that the investment being considered is an investment in the company. Again, in project financing, the investment vehicle may or may not be an entity or a company. It could be an investor financing agreement or a joint-venture agreement (i.e., merely contracts).

Contractual Investment Vehicles

If one or the other of the two contractual investment vehicles are being used (investor financing agreement or joint-venture agreement), it may be appropriate to create a section relating to the company so that information about the production or development company can be provided. In these instances, the filmmaker will want to talk about the nature of the company (i.e., whether it is a sole proprietorship or a general partnership, when it was formed, the location of its offices and who the owners are, at least the controlling owners). For this purpose, the filmmaker may want to use the phrases "wholly owned by" or "majority-owned by," whichever applies. The filmmaker will also want to disclose whether the company is doing business under a fictitious name (dba) and when and where the fictitious name filing occurred. If the company has any history as a business, the filmmaker will want to provide that factual information.

On the other hand, it could also be a corporation yet to be formed or a member-managed LLC now existing or to be formed, both of which are companies but which have little history. Yet again, the filmmaker may have a well-established film-production company that will be used with another investment vehicle and thus will want to provide some discussion relating to that established company, even though the investors will not be directly investing in it. Whatever the circumstances, it is important that the business plan accurately reflect that situation in both the section heading and the text.

Company-Type Investment Vehicles

If one of the company-type investment vehicles is being used (corporation to be formed upon funding or the member-managed LLC), then the investors are actually being asked to invest in the company. In these two instances, it is not misleading to have a "company" section and the information provided for the two investment vehicles in the paragraphs below would also be provided for this company. Once again, the choice of investment vehicle has an impact on what is written throughout the business plan.

As an example, if a filmmaker comes in to see a business-plan consultant and tells the consultant that he or she has already committed to sell the prospective investors a specified percentage of "the company," that is a form of "corporate speak." With corporations and possibly member-managed LLCs, a filmmaker may sell a percentage of the company, but with investor financing agreements and joint ventures, the filmmaker is not selling a percentage of the company. Instead, in those situations, he or she is selling a profit participation in a defined stage of the film's revenue stream. Thus, there are a couple of lessons in this example. One, filmmakers need to be careful about committing to a specific revenue-sharing scheme until certain about which investment vehicle will be used. Secondly, all language used in the business plan must be consistent with that preliminary decision: the choice of investment vehicle and whether that investment vehicle is different than the operating or production company.

Corporation

If the company is a corporation to be formed, the filmmaker will want to disclose the proposed name of the corporation, whether or not the name has been reserved with the secretary of state, in what state the corporation will likely be formed and at what point in the process the corporation will be formed (e.g., upon raising a stated amount of funding). Of course, the basic information relating to the corporation's proposed office address and phone number, if available, should be included. The filmmaker will also want to disclose who among those who are acting as the moving forces behind the formation of this new corporation are expected to be shareholders along with the other investors.

Ownership shares in a corporation can typically be acquired using three different forms of consideration: cash, property or past services. Thus, a filmmaker will also want to disclose, in such instances, what type of consideration is being offered by those involved in promoting the formation of the corporation and who may not be contributing cash. For example, a producer may contribute the rights to a script (property), or the screenwriter may be contributing his or her writing services to date (past services). A film director who is also going to be a corporate shareholder may have contributed his or her consulting services in polishing the script (past services).

Because there are two different types of corporations, the filmmaker may also want to disclose which is likely to be the choice: a regular C corporation or the S corporation, along with the reasons why one may be preferred over the other.[1]

It would also be appropriate to write about the kind of corporate shares to be issued (i.e., whether they are to be voting shares—common stock; or nonvoting, preferred shares). A brief discussion of basic corporate governance may also be included, for example, that initial group of "founding" shareholders will be able to vote at their first annual shareholders' meeting on who will serve on the corporation's initial board of directors, that the board of directors will determine broad policy for the corporation, as well as select the principal corporate officers (e.g., president/CEO, vice-president, secretary/treasurer) and that the corporate officers will run the business on a day-to-day basis, pursuant to board-set policy.

At least one business-plan consultant has suggested in writing that this section ought to disclose whether the corporation is publicly or privately held. Unfortunately, that suggestion is based on the misconception that a business plan can be used in conjunction with the sale of shares in an existing corporation. As noted earlier, if shares in an existing corporation are being offered or sold, the information to be provided to prospective investors must (i.e., is required by law to) take the form of a securities disclosure document, not a business plan. And for the reasons already expressed in chapter 1, a business plan should not even be used as supplemental material in conjunction with a securities offering. That being the case and knowing now that a business plan can only be appropriately used with a corporation to be formed (i.e., its initial incorporation), such a proposed corporation cannot be publicly held (meaning that its securities have been registered with the SEC at the federal level and in each state in which its shares have been sold). Thus, this suggested disclosure is neither needed nor appropriate. It is also quite unfortunate that this sort of misinformation is still floating around out there in the film community.

Member-Managed LLC

If the investment vehicle is an existing member-managed LLC and its operating agreement permits the admission of additional member-managers, a filmmaker will want to disclose in the business plan the name of the member-managed LLC, when its articles of organization were filed with the secretary of state and in which state, who the current and/or original member-managers are and the office address and phone number for the company. A filmmaker will also want to check the state statute pursuant to which the LLC is being formed to see what appropriate consideration (cash, property or services) may be accepted for ownership interests. In some states, consideration for LLC ownership interests is not limited to the more traditional cash, property and past services but may also include future services as consideration for LLC interests (i.e., units). That makes it easier to bring together a group of filmmakers who do not have cash or property to contribute but who can commit to contribute their future services. Further, the filmmaker will want to make sure that provisions are in the LLC's operating agreement that allow the filmmaker to bring in additional member-managers.

If the existing member-managed LLC has any sort of history to report, that should be included in the most factual and straightforward terms. If it has been involved with other film projects in the past, the results of that involvement should be disclosed. The member-managed LLC is more flexible than the corporation as an entity that may be utilized as an investment vehicle for one or more film projects in the sense that its operations are not as formal.

In either case, since the member-managed LLC operates differently than a manager-managed LLC, the filmmaker may want to include a paragraph that explains how the member-managed LLC will operate pursuant to the terms of its proposed or existing operating agreement. Remember, too, that a manager-managed LLC is not an investment-vehicle option when using a business plan because units in a manager-managed LLC are securities, thus a securities disclosure document is required to furnish information to prospective investors in that situation.

The following chart focuses on the essential differences between the various active-investor investment-vehicle options:

	Company	Investment Vehicle	Entity
Investor financing agreement	no	yes	no
Joint-venture agreement	yes	yes	no[1]
Corporation to be formed	yes	yes	yes
Member-managed LLC	yes	yes	yes

NOTE: 1. Joint ventures may be treated as entities for some limited purposes (e.g., taxation).

Mission Statement

In this section of the business plan, a filmmaker may also want to discuss the company's mission (the mission statement). Once again, however, it is not so important for project financing (e.g., financing the costs of producing a single motion picture) to spend much time focusing on the long-term goals of the company or its purpose for existence, which are the traditional functions of a mission statement (unless the company is the same as the investment vehicle). Since mission statements are so closely associated with the long-term future of a company, including a mission statement tends to make prospective investors want to invest in a company, not the single project being promoted through the business plan. So, be aware of this conflict between the long-term goals of a company and the shorter-term goals of the current investment vehicle being promoted through the business plan. Then the filmmaker can place the emphasis where it ought to be in a business plan used for project financing. In other words, a filmmaker does not want to confuse investors by talking so much about the company's long-term mission when the investors are only investing in one of the company's projects.

Business Model

Somewhere in this discussion, a filmmaker may want to talk about the "business model," and if it is unique, why it is unique in the industry in which the filmmaker hopes to operate. Again, for single-film-project financing, the business model may or may not be so unique. It does not have to be. Film finance is not like starting a new business venture that has never been done before. Thousands of filmmakers produce thousands of films each year, and many of them are using the same or similar business models. Of course, lots of filmmakers try to spend a great deal of time and effort coming up with a unique, or what they consider to be a unique, and "trend-setting" approach. But, in truth, the success or failure of their start-up film production companies is based not so much on their business model (which does not have to be unique) as the quality of the first film or films produced. The film or films may be unique, but even then, the film or films may be similar in terms of genre and budget to other films that have already been produced and distributed. This is what allows filmmakers to gather information about films of a similar budget and genre to create a box-office comparables section for the business plan.

Thus, independent-film finance appears to be one of those situations in which business plans may not need to follow the more traditional approaches created by business-plan consultants and authors for business plans using the corporate structure or a product other than film. And, of course, the use of the business plan to raise money from a few active investors is not a unique business model.

Overall Strategy

It may also be appropriate and helpful to discuss overall strategy for the company or project. That may include the nature of the company, the investment vehicle, the type of film, how the filmmaker hopes to produce it, how he or she hopes to get a distribution deal, how it may be distributed and so forth. In effect, however, the entire business plan is an expression of the filmmaker's strategy. So, the summary of the business plan may be the best place to discuss strategy, based on the assumption that almost everything else in the business plan is a component of this overall strategy.

Strategic Relationships

Some business-plan consultants recommend that this section relating to the company include a discussion of something called "strategic relationships." Filmmakers sometimes try to include the names of important people in the industry whom they know or companies they hope to do business with. Those are not strategic relationships. That is more like name-dropping, which may be considered dishonest or misleading.

In the context of business dealings, the term relationship implies that the filmmaker's company is already (currently) engaged in business dealings with the other company. If that is not the case, do not state, suggest or imply that it is. The relationship is strategic if it is necessary or important to the initiation, conduct or completion of a plan. For example, certainly if a production company has an output deal with a distributor, that would be considered a strategic relationship. Distribution is necessary and important to the conduct and completion of the plan to distribute the film. And, if the filmmaker's company has an ongoing contractual relationship with that distributor, that is the kind of relationship that will work. If not, do not write anything that will suggest a business relationship that does not actually exist. Personal relationships ("industry contacts") are not sufficient for this purpose. Some hint of such personal relationship may be provided in the narrative biographies by factually naming some of the people the filmmaker has worked with on other film projects. But do not talk about the quality of the relationship (i.e., the producer has strong personal relationships with so-and-so). That's not appropriate. It's too subjective and speculative.

On the other hand, it may be appropriate to create a listing of some of the existing distribution companies and describe several of the films they have distributed in the past as an indication of the specific distributor market to which the filmmaker anticipates marketing his or her film once it is completed. Just be very clear about the fact that no distribution agreement is currently in place. If it is a fact that the filmmaker has had some preliminary discussions with certain film-distribution companies about distributing the filmmaker's film, and they, in fact, expressed interest in seeing the film once it is completed, then the filmmaker may state that fact. However, in that instance, it may be safer not to name the companies unless the filmmaker actually has letters of intent or interest, regardless of the contingencies involved.

Geographic Scope of Venture

It may also be appropriate to briefly disclose in the company section of the business plan the proposed geographic scope of the planned business venture. If the plan is to produce one or more feature films for a theatrical release, that geographic scope is likely to be worldwide, although other possible distribution options may be discussed in the distribution section.

This "company" or "investment vehicle" section of the business plan is not the place to provide much information beyond goals, objectives or mission statements regarding what the company is going to do. The information relating more directly to the film or film project is reserved for another major section of the business plan: "The Products" or "The Films," whichever the filmmaker chooses to name that section (see chapter 7).

Sample Company/Investment-Vehicle Section

The Company/Investment Vehicle

This investment opportunity is being created to finance, produce and arrange for the distribution of a single Motion Picture. The Picture will be a low-budget theatrical feature that the Producers believe will require lower revenues to recoup the investment than higher-budgeted films. Thus, management has intentionally determined to produce a low-budget theatrical feature based upon the belief that such strategy offers a greater likelihood of financial success for it and its Investor(s). Furthermore, Management believes that by operating outside the Hollywood studio system, it will be more likely to create a Film of a unique nature and merit that would therefore have an advantage at the box office.

The organization providing the impetus for the fund-raising activity associated with this business plan is an existing California corporation, wholly owned by the individual filmmaker Wilbur Smith. The corporation is not offering its shares by means of this business plan, rather it is seeking opportunities to partner with joint-venture partners or to bring in dedicated investors through one or a few investor financing agreements. Even so, the corporation was formed in August of 2007, and its corporate offices are located at 2345 Wilshire Boulevard, Suite 304, Los Angeles, California 90124; phone (310) 477-8282. Since its incorporation, the corporation has been involved in the acquisition of underlying rights and the development of scripts suitable for production.

The Management of XYZ Productions Inc. will be significantly involved in all decisions with respect to the financing and production of the Picture, as well as certain important decisions relating to the Film's distribution. The Active

Investor(s) (or Joint-Venture Partner[s]) providing funding for the Picture will also take part in the control of the project's business and in the production of the Picture and thus will have certain rights or authority as more specifically set out in the Investor Financing Agreement, Joint-Venture Agreement or other financing-vehicle documentation. Such Investor(s) will have only such rights and powers as such Investor(s) are expressly provided in such agreement but will have to be regularly involved in helping to make important decisions with respect to the project in order to maintain their active-investor status. In order to qualify as active investors, such persons will also have to demonstrate that they have knowledge and experience in the film industry.

5. Management: People Committed to the Project

Once again, we first have to ask, "Does this section have to be entitled 'Management'?" which is the traditional corporate-type business-plan title for this section dealing with the people involved. The answer is "No." In fact, under some circumstances using the term "Management" as the title of this major section in a business plan could be confusing or misleading. For example, if the investment vehicle is a member-managed LLC, and the filmmaker wants to include the narrative biography of a film's proposed director or director of photography, but such individuals are not involved in any way in the ownership or management of the investment vehicle or the production company, then it would be inappropriate to include their biographical information in a section entitled "Management." They are not management of the company. On the other hand, they play critical roles in the production of a feature film and its potential for success, so including their bios is likely to be very important to prospective investors.

Some business-plan consultants suggest that the information relating to management be included as a subsection for the major section called "The Company" (see chapter 4). But for film-related business plans, especially for a start-up operation, there may be so little information to disclose about a company that treating "Management" as a company subsection would not make sense.

The section title "Management" is more appropriate for a corporate investment vehicle to be formed upon funding; the very likely the reason why most business-plan consultants recommend the use of this section heading is because they are used to using the corporation as the investment vehicle. On the other hand, some of the people involved in the development, production or distribution of a feature-film project, whose bios need to be included for review by prospective investors, are not involved with the corporation as management. They are independent contractors who are going to be hired to help perform specific services with respect to the film project once the project is funded.

For these reasons, it may better serve the needs of film-related business plans to use another title for this important section. As an example, "People of the XYZ LLC" may work when a member-managed LLC is the investment vehicle. In the alternative, "People of (title of the film)" may work when some of the people are not involved as owners or management of the particular entity, but letting the prospective investors know who is involved and who may be making significant contributions to the project is still essential. Such titles are broader in scope than the title "Management" and may work better for that reason for the section with the narrative biographies of the key people associated with the project. So again, when writing a business plan for the project financing of a film, it is important to adapt to the special circumstances of feature-film development and/or production—it is common for independent films to hire numerous professionals as independent contractors or temporary employees solely for the purpose of developing or producing a specific film.

This section is important for raising money for film projects because investors tend to rely heavily on the backgrounds of the key people involved when making a decision to invest in any start-up venture, and a filmmaker must convince these prospective investors that he or she not only knows which pieces of the puzzle need to be brought together in order to produce a quality film but also that he or she has actually identified and communicated with several of those key people, and they have expressed interest in lending their expertise to the project.

Whose biographical information ought to be included in a film-related business plan? People functioning as executive producers, coproducers, associate producers, line producers or production managers, screenwriters, directors, directors of photography, actors and casting directors are typically some of the narrative biographies seen in business plans relating to a film project. These choices also depend on who is the moving force behind the project. If a stunt person, as an example, is seeking to put together the financing for a film project, he or she may also serve as a producer, owner of the production company and in a stunt supervisor's role. Any person involved in the development, production or distribution of a motion picture may decide at some point in their careers to become a proactive entrepreneur (i.e., the entrepreneurial producer) and seek to finance the development, production and/or distribution of a particular film project with which they are going to be involved.

Others, sometimes listed as consultants, may include entertainment attorneys, securities attorneys, accountants, production accounting firms, marketing consultants and script doctors. Some of these individuals may also double as management for the production or development company, thus their biographies may list them by their management title as well as their expected screen credit.

A weak management section is often cited as one of the more critical business-plan mistakes. Obviously, if the biographies of the people associated with the project do not have a background that suggests they have the ability to deliver on the film project described, that will not be encouraging to prospective investors. So, if a filmmaker is not experienced enough to persuade prospective investors that he or she is capable of successfully completing such a project, he or she may want to surround themselves with (i.e., attach) others with more experience. This assessment requires some objectivity on the part of the people who are the moving forces behind the business venture. They must step back and ask, "Will my prospective investors be impressed with the backgrounds of the individuals whose bios appear in the management section of this business plan?" If not, it is time to get out and recruit more people with more impressive and relevant backgrounds to supplement the team already in place. This is one of the questions a filmmaker may want to ask of outside advisers (i.e., those the filmmaker asks to review the business plan as it goes through its various drafts).

As filmmakers all recognize, the production of a feature film is a collaborative process. That means a lot of people are typically involved in the production of a feature film for theatrical release. For this reason, it is a good idea to include the biographies of a fair selection of the people the filmmaker intends to be involved in helping to produce the film so that investors can be assured that this group as a whole has the expertise to produce a quality motion picture. The underlying but unstated assumption relating to their bios is that since they have worked on many other feature films, they know what they are doing. On the other hand, many of these people, as noted above, will not be committed to the project as owners of the production company or even as management, and it is difficult to obtain a firm commitment from many of such individuals without the production financing being in place. In film parlance, this activity is referred to as attaching elements to the script to create a film package.

So, at what point is it fair to disclose their possible involvement? The filmmaker's first obligation to investors is to be honest. Do not mislead investors about the involvement of anyone. But, it is fair to state the facts. For example, if the filmmaker has talked to a well-known director, he or she has read the script, the director has expressed an interest in directing the picture contingent upon the filmmaker raising the production financing, the director's compensation is mutually agreed upon, and no other contractual commitments of the director would conflict with the start date on which the filmmaker needs the director's services, there is no reason why the filmmaker cannot disclose these same facts (with the director's permission) at the end of the proposed director's narrative bio in the business plan. These are the same or similar contingencies that would be set out in a letter of intent from this director or anyone from whom the filmmaker is able to obtain a letter of intent. If a letter of intent from this director is included the letter as an exhibit to the business plan, the filmmaker would simply be summarizing the contents of the letter of intent as part of the narrative bio of the director in the main body of the business plan. The statement about the actual state of the relationship and commitment must be accurate.

Order of Biographies

Generally, the owner/management biographies would precede the purely creative personnel. More specifically, if the production company is a sole proprietorship, the bio of the owner of the production company would most likely be the first narrative biography. If a corporation is wholly owned by a few individuals, their bios would appear early. If the entity is a member-managed LLC, the member-manager bios would come first. The other titles, such as prospective screen credits, for these same individuals would be included with that individual's descriptive header. After the owner/management, film-related bios typically are those of the producers, screenwriter, director, director of photography (if available), actors and others. A separate section "Consultants" may follow, including biographies for attorneys, accountants, third-party business-plan consultants and financial-projection consultants.

Narrative Biography versus Résumé

Some business-plan consultants recommend that a very short (maybe one- or two-paragraph) summary of a résumé be included in the body of the business plan, and the complete resumés be inserted as exhibits. Aside from possibly wasting trees for the extra paper, creating redundancy and adding unnecessary length to the overall business plan, this approach is not investor friendly. After all, a filmmaker does not want to make investors look for information in two different places if just looking at one place can suffice.

Of course, a little more work is involved in preparing narrative biographies that adequately cover the subject, and some writing skill is required. Narrative biographies tell the story of the professional life of an individual as opposed to the resumé style, which does not necessarily use complete sentences, is organized by topics and typically uses a bullet-point format.

Drafting Tips

Some suggestions for writing a narrative biography for a film-related business plan are:

A filmmaker may want to stress to the individuals providing their bios for inclusion in the business plan that they should eliminate the puffery in advance, and if they do not, the filmmaker should do that for them. Of course, that can create a bit of tension between the writer of the business plan and the individuals providing their bios; after all, some have major egos, and they have worked hard to draft their own bios the way they want them. Unfortunately, excellence in one field, like film production, does not necessarily carry over as excellence in another field, like writing narrative biographies for a business plan. The individuals are also subjectively involved in their bios. But, it is the filmmaker's business plan, and the filmmaker is trying to raise money for a project through the use of this business plan. So, if it is not professional, and the prospective investors are not impressed, the filmmaker loses. Thus, a filmmaker needs to be prepared to assert his or her priority to create the most professional, accurate and informative business plan by being willing to fight that little fight over who controls the final form of the biography that is going into the business plan.

In the bio itself, start with the name of the individual in bold, upper-case letters set against the left margin. Center his or her relevant professional titles and film credits, for example: "Producer and LLC Member/Manager" or "Screenwriter and Director" or "Actor and Owner of the Production Company."

Using full justification, create an introductory sentence that summarizes this person's professional life, for example, "James Edwards has been involved in the film industry as a screenwriter, director and producer for fifteen years." Be sure that this introductory sentence is accurate based on the biographical information that follows in the bio.

Add the detail that supports the introductory sentence. Some use a chronological approach here, but it may be preferable to start with the most recent and relevant work experience and present the information in reverse order, based on the assumption that the individual's most recent experience is the more relevant to the business plan. Of course, that is not always true. Someone may have done something a few years back that makes him or her most qualified to work on this film project in a specific capacity. If that is the case, the filmmaker would want to start this person's bio with the most relevant information since many readers may be just skimming the bios at first.

In any case and once again using the SEC disclosure guidelines as a useful (although not required) model for presenting business-plan information, include the person's work experience at least for the last five years, along with names of the companies worked for, the dates and the individual's titles, responsibilities and significant accomplishments. Again, stay away from the exaggeration, and just stick with the facts.

If the individual has film credits, in addition to listing the names of films, include the date of release, the name of the distributor, names of the film's stars if the filmmaker wants, the screen credit obtained by that individual on that film, the names of other key people the individual worked with (e.g., the name of the director) and so forth. Typically a director of photography would want to include the names of the directors with which he or she has worked. Actors may want to include the names of directors with which they have worked. Producers may want to include the names of other producers or executive producers with whom they have worked. Similarly, a filmmaker may want to include the names of the distributors for the films on which an individual has worked.

Three or four paragraphs of factual information covering the individual's professional career should be adequate. Including some information about the charity work the individual has been involved with, if any, may be appropriate. But, do not get too personal; do not include information about hobbies or other favorite activities.

The sentence or two about a person's education goes well in a small, next-to-last paragraph in the bio (which follows with the reverse chronological approach, being some of the last information provided). Stay away from high school and just list the relevant education after high school, such as colleges attended or degrees earned. Although a minor point, avoid saying someone "has" a degree from some university. Why not be more accurate and state that he or she "earned a BS in Communications from the University of Utah in 1987"? The college graduate probably would appreciate that. Some individuals will not have earned a degree but may have attended college and studied in a specific area, may have taken relevant courses through extension offices or other similar programs or may have attended some of the many film-industry-related seminar presentations provided around the country each year. That information may be described in the person's bio.

A good way to end the bio is with a short sentence, for example, "At age thirty-four (or whatever the person's age), Mr. So and So resides with his family in Such and Such City." That wraps up the biographical information and tends to add credibility to the individual, since business plans are often presented to people all over the country or world, and providing a location helps the prospective investors understand where people are situated. Stay away from including the names and number of children, if any, or the spouse, if any, because there is simply a feeling that such information is too personal. Also, the actual age of the individual is not required for a business plan, whereas for some securities disclosure documents, it is required for the key people. Further, a filmmaker may experience some resistance from some individuals with respect to disclosing their age, particularly those who have been lying about their age for years (this actually occurred with a client), or just do not feel it is anyone's business. On the other hand, a filmmaker may want to take the position (as the SEC does) that prospective investors have a right to know how old (and experienced) these people are because the investors are being asked to provide financing for an important business venture in which these individuals are playing a significant role.

Some Recommended Don'ts

It is not recommended starting a bio by reciting where someone was born and discussing where he or she grew up. Such information is not likely to be very relevant to a film project being developed or produced by adults asking for other adults to invest their money, except in those few instances where the script is based on the person's childhood experiences. In those cases, it may be relevant to state somewhere in the bio that the person wrote the script and it is somewhat autobiographical, but that is still not the information with which to begin a bio. If the script is not only about a particular town from which the producer hails, and the producer intends on raising a significant amount of money to produce the film in that town, it may make sense to include the fact that the producer is a native of such and such town, but otherwise, just skip origins and childhood experiences.

Similarly, stay away from providing information about individuals that goes all the way back to high school, middle school or even elementary school. This is a business plan, and the prospective investors are typically more interested in what this individual has done since becoming an adult. Telling the investors that a person started shooting little films as a child is not that useful or impressive. Including such information in a business plan biography is more likely to suggest to prospective investors that a filmmaker is trying to pursue a childhood dream and asking someone else to pay for it.

Stay away from using the first names of the individual in the body of the bio, even if that person is the filmmaker's best friend. It is more professional to prospective investors, who may or may not know these individuals, to refer to them as Mr. So-and-So or Ms. So-and-So or Mrs. So-and-So, as the case may be. Then the wording can vary with "he" or "she" from time to time.

When monitoring the language used and avoiding the puffery, exaggeration, flowery language and hyperbole typically associated with the writing of public-relations professionals and so common in the film industry, keep the following caveats in mind. These are taken from actual client-provided biographical information.

Don't make subjective statements like, "His education benefitted him tremendously in his directorial approach, thus aiding his storytelling techniques." That's someone's opinion; just replace it with the factual statement, "He earned a film degree with a concentration on writing at the University of Southern California in 1998."

Do not refer to any film school as "prestigious." That again, is a matter of opinion. Just leave it out. Give the name of the film school, the years attended, whether he or she graduated, with honors, if any, and what the major or concentration was.

Avoid the speculative and subjective statements like, "He quickly excelled in the producing program and earned the respect and trust of the faculty." Instead, if he produced a film short while in school, state the facts about that.

Don't provide the opinion "The film was a phenomenal success!" Instead, state the facts about where and when the film was screened, what awards it won, how big an audience saw it, how much money it earned or other factual information.

Don't say a filmmaker won a "nationally renowned" scholarship. Just say he or she won a scholarship, provide the name of the scholarship, what it was awarded for, what the prize consisted of and the date. Again, just provide the facts.

Don't offer the opinion that someone is a "respected producer." Just say he or she is a producer, and recite his or her producing experience as factually as possible.

Don't say someone is "passionate about their work." Who knows how they feel inside?

Don't state that someone has "maintained strong relationships in the entertainment industry." A bio is not written for the purpose of stating things that cannot be demonstrated. If he or she worked with someone on a specific project, name the project, with whom they worked and when. Those are facts. Nobody really knows whether those people still have a "strong relationship." That part is entirely subjective.

Don't say someone worked on a film that was "wildly successful." What does that mean? Wildly successful for whom: the distributor, the production company, the investors or an actor? Nobody really knows. If the film won awards, state that. If the film did well at the box office, cite the facts. Avoid the vague exaggeration.

Sample Narrative Biographies
Jim Noble

DIRECTOR/COWRITER/PRODUCER

ORIGINAL MEMBER-MANAGER OF LLC

Jim Noble is originally from Springfield, Illinois, the principal planned location for shooting the Film. He has developed the feature Script *All Alone with Me* based on the award-winning short story *Tell Me How It Is* by Springfield author Stan Donner. Mr. Noble is slated to direct.

Mr. Noble also produced the just-completed feature film *Travel On*, which will be released by Excellent Distributor in late 2010 or early 2011. The film stars Dave Jarrott (*Tame, Quiet Days, Don't Look, South of Dakota* and *Green for Me*) along with Tom Elliott (*Talk, BET Comedy* and *The Price Is Right*). This contemporary Asian *Torn Rider* tells the story of two San Francisco gangbangers who abandon their past, zooming cross-country on Ninja-style motorcycles seeking a fresh start in life. The soundtrack features original tracks by Pearl Jam, Troubadour, Elvis Presley, Marshall and others.

Mr. Noble cowrote and directed "Bloomfield," the pilot episode of the *Farm House* series, which won the Grand Jury Prize at Worldfest/Houston, a Silver Plaque at the Toronto International Film Festival, the Audience Favorite Award at the Colorado Film Festival and a Cine Golden Eagle. He created and produced Epiphany's Showtime series *Farm House*, which won two Cable Ace Awards and an Emmy, along with other nominations. The series was executive produced by Nathan Johanson. Episodes were directed by Nathan Johanson, Jeannie Bodeman, Peter Randall, George Rashall, Bill Wind and Gerald McCauley. The series has featured actors Barbara Hunt, Ray Field, Kathleen Ford, George Prime, Brooke Jade, Dan Joseph and Michael Tabold. The "Three Little Girls" episode premiered as an official selection at the Telluride Film Festival.

He also produced the feature film *Torn*, distributed by 20th Century Fox. This film presented an unflinching portrait of a teenage mother cast out upon the mean streets of Miami. It was partially subsidized by grants from the AFI and the NEA. In addition, Mr. Noble served as a producer/writer/director on the fourteen-episode PBS television series *Fantastic: The Last Appeal*. The series was hosted by James Biddle and was produced by XYZ Entertainment, in conjunction with Rolling Along Pictures.

Mr. Noble earned his BA in Communications/Visual Arts from the University of Arkansas. At the University of California Los Angeles (UCLA) School of Theater, Film and Television graduate school, he directed the award-winning short *Train That Tiger*, distributed by Tame Home Entertainment.

At age thirty-three, Mr. Noble resides in Pacific Palisades, California.

Carl French
PRODUCER/MANAGER OF PRODUCTION

Carl French is an award-winning writer, director and producer of feature films, television series and documentaries, along with corporate educational and training films.

He served as a producer on the 2003 feature *Red Hogs* and also produced the film's compilation soundtrack CD. Previously, he worked as the Supervising Producer, Creator and Writer on the NBC series *Real People* (1999–2002) and as the Creator and Producer for the Showtime series *Wall Street* (1993–98). Mr. French was the Producer for the pilot leading to the Showtime series *Fort Knox Blues* (*Teledyne*, 1995), and he produced the 35 mm film short *Journey* (1991) starring Robert Bodine.

In the early 1990s, Mr. French served as the President of Certain Entertainment, a creative-development/production company. He was the Writer/Editor on the NBC children's series *Will I Ever Grow Up* (1993–97), and he was the Executive Vice-President for Creative Development for *Drunks* (Journey Inc., 1991–92) starring Rachel George, Dean Russell and Jerry Basalt. Among other projects in the late 1980s, he produced and directed Cheryl Subsidy, Jimmy George and Rhonda in *Formula: The Real Deal*. He has also written two screenplays.

Mr. French's *Portobello: Lost in China* (1998) received an Emmy and a Cable Ace Award. In 1999, he won a Cine Golden Eagle and Special Gold Jury Award at the Denver Film Festival and Silver Plaque at the Seattle Film Festival for *Geraldine*.

On the corporate side, Mr. French has produced, directed and written industrial films, training films and educational programs for Ford, Bank of America, Teledyne, Lehman Bros., San Diego State University and others.

Mr. French studied film and television at Bullard University. He earned his BFA degree in Film/TV from the Florida State University in 1985.

6. Market Overview/State of the Industry

Once again, a variety of titles might work for this major section of a business plan, including "The Market," "Description of Business" and "Plan of Business," although each implies a slightly different bit of information. "The Market" and "Market Overview/State of the Industry" suggest that the discussion will be about the marketplace itself and not about the venture's actual plans. That's saved for another section. The section headings "Description of Business" and "Plan of Business" imply that some of the discussion may include material that is more specific to the proposed venture for which funding is being sought. Try to avoid calling this section "Business Plan" because that's what the entire document is called, and using the same title for both is confusing. It is important to think through the proposed titles for these major sections and to not rely on the section headings used by others for their business plans because significant differences may exist between the model previously used and the plan under construction.

Assuming for purposes of this book that funding is being sought for a single feature film, this section first should provide factual statistical information with a discussion about the market in which the proposed venture will seek to compete (i.e., in this case, the film industry). It is acceptable to discuss the major studio/distributors because even an independently produced movie could possibly be acquired for distribution by one of the majors, even though the odds are not that favorable.

Typically, the text of this section starts with a discussion supported by current statistics for the broader marketplace (i.e., the film industry generally) annual box-office earnings of the industry, market share, number of films produced or released, which companies are the most important participants, the source material for scripts, genre and rating information and movie-attendance figures. Much of this kind of statistical information can be obtained from the Motion Picture Association of America (MPAA) Web site and that of the National Association of

Theatre Owners.[1] Information relating to one or more of the ancillary markets for the film may be discussed, usually in the order in which such markets are likely to be exploited. If available, studies relating to market trends and revenue streams may also be included along with citations to the sources for such information, although specific references to how the film may perform in the marketplace should be reserved for the box-office comparables section (showing how similar films have performed) and/or the financial projections (see "Box-office comparables," chapter 7, and chapter 10). Keep in mind that the information reported in the box-office comparables section is looking to the past. The information reported in the financial projections is looking to the future.

A subsection providing a brief overview of the independent sector of the film industry, both from historical and contemporary perspectives, would be appropriate (assuming the subject film project is an independent film). Because of its prominence among independent-film festivals, information regarding the kinds of films competing and film-acquisition activity for the most recent several years of the Sundance Film Festival may also prove to be instructive.

To avoid reporting only positive information and being one-sided, some negative information about the industry, such as the latest statistics relating to movie piracy and how competitive the industry is should also be included.

A separate and specific subsection relating to the competition to be faced by the project for which funding is being sought might be the most appropriate approach. This may consist of a discussion of the reported activities of other independent-film development and production companies, the films they have recently produced and had distributed, available information about how successful such films have been, along with the producer's strategy for competing in this specific segment of the marketplace.

If the film is intended to appeal to a specific target audience (e.g., a children's film or faith-based audience), general statistical information regarding that audience may be included. However, this subsection has a somewhat different focus as opposed to the target-audience analysis that should more appropriately appear in the major section of the business plan dealing with "The Product" or "The Film Project" (see chapter 7). This section is about the marketplace generally, even though it may contain some specific information and/or statistics about the type of film being considered.

A producer may also want to include a broader discussion of film finance in this section and how various forms of film finance relate to film distribution. A section on distribution options and relating to the functions of distributors may also be included, as the following examples illustrate.

Distributor revenue streams. It would be appropriate to include any available statistical data representing average percentages for each of the possible film-revenue streams in a discussion relating to distribution. There may be other sources for such information, but Paul Kagan Associates prepares what the company refers to as media studies showing the entertainment revenues forecast for entertainment media distributors from time to time (see table 6.6). The table in the sample section is a combination of two Paul Kagan Associates reports with the percentages recalculated to show the percentage based on worldwide revenues. The source of such data must be cited.

Research services/collections and databases. More-detailed information about the film industry is available currently than ten years ago. Much of the change was brought about by the development and widespread use of the Internet and the opportunities it presents to analyze revenue streams from statistical information and databases. Unfortunately, for researchers, much of this information is available only at a price. In addition, some of the more important factual information regarding the film industry, such as the background information on the top-level studio executives, needed for purposes of analyzing the level of or lack of diversity at the top in the industry, is not readily available.[2]

A sample "Market Overview/State of the Industry" section for a business plan for the film industry might include some of the following types of information updated for the most-current year available. Various subsections of this example were borrowed from several different types of film offerings; thus, clearly not all of this information will apply to any single future film project. The business-plan preparer must exercise reasonable judgment as to what sections may still apply in terms of time and content to the current project being promoted through the filmmaker's business plan.

Sample "Market Overview/State of the Industry"
Market Overview/State of the Industry

Movie ticket sales for 2008 came in at $9.63 billion, ahead of the $9.62 billion earned in 2007. Admissions were down roughly 4 percent, far less than declines in other sectors of the U.S. economy. During the year, twenty-four titles grossed more than $100 million, almost as many as in 2007. Each of the six major studios all matched or improved on their 2007 box-office results. Each exceeded the $1 billion mark in ticket sales. Combined, the majors released 148 pictures versus 160 in 2007. [Source: "Box Office Resists Recession," *Variety*, January 4, 2009].

Ticket sales at North American movie theaters totaled $9.6 billion in 2008, a decrease of less than 1 percent over 2007, according to Media by Numbers, a box-office-tracking company. Attendance declined 5 percent, to about 1.3 billion. [Source: (Brooks Barnes, "Hollywood's Superheroes Save the Day," *New York Times*, January 5, 2009.)

The Hollywood-based major studio/distributors saw 2008 foreign grosses rise 4 percent and set a new record of $9.9 billion. Amid a worldwide recession, the gain underlines the durability of the international film business, at least for the major studios. Those studios have seen a 15 percent hike in foreign box office over the past two years. [Source: "Foreign Grosses Rise to New Record," *Variety*, January 4, 2009]

2007 film-industry statistics. The domestic box office total for 2007 was $9.62 billion, the best year on record. The figure represents a 5 percent gain over 2006 and a 4 percent increase over the previous highest year of 2002. Admissions, however, were up only 1 percent over 2006 and were down when compared to 2002. The total number of films released in the United States in 2007 remained on par with 2006 with 603 films released. Domestic theater admissions held steady at 1.4 billion tickets in 2007. In 2007, the top-grossing films offered more diverse fare in terms of ratings, with a 50 percent increase in both PG- and R-rated films. The average cost to make and market a major MPAA member company film was $106.6 million in 2007. This includes $70.8 million in negative costs and $35.9 million in marketing costs. In 2007, the average price of a movie ticket in the United States rose to $6.88, a 5 percent increase over 2006. [Source: www.mpaa.org.]

In another first, all six of the major studio/distributors reached the $1 billion mark at the domestic box office. Market share among the majors is shown in table 6.1.

Table 6.1.
Market share and percentage increase of domestic box office
of the major studio/distributors in 2007

Rank	Studio	2007 box office receipts ($ million)	Change in 2007 box office receipts from 2006 (%)
1	Paramount	1,490	+55
2	Warner Bros.	1,420	+34
3	Disney	1,360	−9
4	Sony	1,240	−27
5	Universal	1,100	+38
6	20th Century Fox	1,010	−28
7	New Line	485	+93
8	Lionsgate	368	+11
9	MGM	363	+122

SOURCE: Pamela McClintock, "2007 Films Hit Record Box Office," *Variety*, January 2, 2008.

The foreign box office for 2007 also reached record levels. Seven tent pole pictures combined for nearly $3.5 billion, and the six major-studio distributors saw their offshore grosses jump 9 percent to $9.4 billion [Source: Dave McNary, "Foreign Box Office Hits Record Levels," *Variety*, January 1, 2008]. Worldwide box office reached another all-time high in 2007 with $26.7 billion, a 4.9 percent increase. [Source: www.mpaa.org].

Among the studio specialty divisions, total box-office receipts for 2007 were down 4 percent from 2006. The top fifteen specialty units and independent distributors, including MGM and the Weinstein Company, posted domestic box-office receipts of $1.03 billion, down slightly from the $1.04 billion in 2006 (see table 6.2).

Table 6.2.
Total receipts in domestic box office in 2006 and 2007

Distributor	2006 total receipts ($ million)	2007 total receipts ($ million)	Percentage change in 2007 from 2006 (%)
Searchlight	161.2	136.2	−18
Miramax	46.2	125.4	+171
Focus	180.2	124.8	−44
Paramount Vantage/Classics	46.5	60.9	+30
Picturehouse	24.0	58.3	+142
Sony Pictures Classics	59.7	37.8	−57
Warner Independent	27.4	15.0	−75

SOURCE: www.mpaa.org.

Annual ticket sales. Table 6.3 sets out the number of movie tickets sold in the United States (in the billions) and the corresponding revenue figure for each year (in the billions of dollars).

Table 6.3.
Annual ticket sales and revenue in the United States, 1995–2008

Year	Tickets (billion)	Revenue ($ billion)
1995	1.21	5.26
1996	1.30	5.77
1997	1.36	6.23
1998	1.44	6.74
1999	1.46	7.36
2000	1.38	7.42
2001	1.44	8.12
2002	1.61	9.34
2003	1.53	9.25
2004	1.49	9.28
2005	1.38	8.85
2006	1.42	9.28
2007	1.40	9.60
2008	1.33	9.17

SOURCE: "US Movie Market Summary 1995–2009," *Nash Information Services,* http://www.the-numbers.com/market; MPAA.

Genres, ratings and sources. When it comes to the source of hit movies, scripts written on spec and based on original ideas have continued to dominate the box office. More than one hundred spec scripts topped the list as the source of the annual top-grossing movies over the last ten years. Scripts based on books placed second at forty. Table 6.4 provides statistical information relating to movie genres, MPAA ratings and sources. In the view of the Producers, such statistics suggest that they have chosen a movie genre, MPAA rating and source that statistically has the greatest potential for box-office performance. NO ASSURANCES CAN BE PROVIDED THAT SUCH STATISTICAL ANALYSIS WILL BEAR ANY RELATIONSHIP TO THE BOX-OFFICE PERFORMANCE OF THE LLC'S FILM PROJECT.

Home video. Despite unit sales being up, consumer spending on home video declined this year. Preliminary projections for overall spending on all video rentals and sales in the United States for 2005 indicate a drop of less than 1 percent from $24.1 billion of 2004, according to *DVD Exclusive* (a sister publication of *Daily Variety*). Among the factors for the overall decline of the home-video market to $24 billion are: the continued collapse of VHS—down roughly 60 percent in 2005 to about $1.5 billion, or just 6 percent of the overall home-video market; a 4 percent decline in the overall $7.78 billion rental market, which has been sliding since its peak of $8.4 billion in 2001; rapidly falling DVD retail prices; the continued growth of TV DVDs whose many hours of content keep consumers satisfied longer between purchases; and top titles not reaching the same heights—only one title topped $230 million in 2005. In 2004, there were three, two of which exceeded $300 million.

Despite the 1 percent decline in revenue of the entire home-video market, total spending on DVDs alone was up to $22 billion, a near 10 percent jump from 2004. [Source: Scott Hettrick, "Spending on DVDs up 10%," *Variety.com*, December 29, 2005]. Furthermore, with the number of DVD units shipped expected to jump from 715 million to 1.5 billion in the upcoming years, consumer spending on DVDs is expected to more than double to $51 billion by 2008. [Source: Michael Learmonth, "Aud Spending Spike—Surprise Hits Expected to Push B.O. Up 10%," *Variety.com*, August 1, 2004].

PricewaterhouseCoopers study. According to studies by PricewaterhouseCoopers, 88 percent of U.S. households had DVD players in 2008. With $7.7 billion in rental income taken into consideration, consumers will spend nearly four times more money on movies and TV shows on disc than they do at the box office by the end of the decade. The predictions are part of PricewaterhouseCoopers' annual "Global Entertainment and Media Outlook" review of consumer and intra-industry spending in all media.

The report states that the continued DVD sales boom predicted for the next three to five years will be due largely to the addition of more than 40 million DVD households in the United States alone. That kind of hardware expansion should more than double the volume of DVD units shipped, from around 715 million units today to 1.5 billion within the next five years, which is expected to more than double the $22 billion currently spent by DVD consumers today.

Table 6.4.

Top-grossing movies by genre, MPAA rating, movie source, movie production method, and creative type, 1995–2008

Category with movie rank	Genre or Rating	Number of movies	Total gross ($)	Average gross ($)	Market share (%)
Genre					
1	Comedy	1,423	33,610,222,557	23,619,271	24.79
2	Adventure	415	26,320,487,549	63,422,862	19.42
3	Drama	2,462	25,482,057,278	10,350,145	18.80
4	Action	434	22,659,182,352	52,210,098	16.71
5	Thriller/suspense	390	8,835,725,037	22,655,705	6.52
6	Romantic comedy	303	7,893,674,425	26,051,731	5.82
7	Horror	260	6,601,205,482	25,389,252	4.87
8	Musical	115	1,490,089,086	12,957,296	1.10
9	Documentary	687	1,288,340,049	1,875,313	0.95
10	Black comedy	59	605,386,253	10,260,784	0.45
11	Western	31	445,219,399	14,361,916	0.33
12	Concert/performance	36	161,367,655	4,482,435	0.12
13	Multiple genres	11	2,703,943	245,813	0.00
14	Genre unknown	5	1,475,120	295,024	0.00
MPAA rating					
1	PG-13	1,519	60,596,291,048	39,892,226	44.74
2	R	2,773	40,667,928,664	14,665,679	30.03
3	PG	766	24,983,638,643	32,615,716	18.45
4	G	231	7,687,132,511	33,277,630	5.68
5	Not rated (NR)	722	1,084,263,617	1,501,750	0.80
6	NC-17	16	51,863,291	3,241,456	0.04
7	Open	5	6,728,826	1,345,765	0.00
Movie source					
1	Original screenplay	3,278	57,792,638,251	17,630,457	42.67
2	Based on book/ short story	1,092	27,197,217,191	24,905,877	20.08
3	Sequel	307	20,321,407,283	66,193,509	15.00
4	Remake	170	7,825,345,361	46,031,443	5.78
5	Based on real-life events	983	7,490,945,658	7,620,494	5.53
6	Based on TV	116	5,436,773,353	46,868,736	4.01
7	Based on comic/ graphic novel	66	4,134,784,939	62,648,257	3.05
8	Based on play	151	1,295,516,246	8,579,578	0.96
9	Traditional/legend/ fairytale	24	769,427,469	32,059,478	0.57
10	Based on musical/opera	26	725,419,247	27,900,740	0.54
11	Based on game	18	566,578,409	31,476,578	0.42
12	Disney Ride	5	454,932,425	90,986,485	0.34
13	Spin-off	10	437,240,340	43,724,034	0.32

Table 6.4. (continued)

Category with movie rank	Genre or Rating	Number of movies	Total gross ($)	Average gross ($)	Market share (%)
14	Based on magazine article	10	394,501,904	39,450,190	0.29
15	Based on short film	13	307,550,909	23,657,762	0.23
16	Musical-group movie	1	43,044,142	43,044,142	0.03
17	Based on toy	1	17,657,974	17,657,974	0.01
18	Compilation	11	6,298,124	572,557	0.00
19	Based on ballet	2	1,442,261	721,131	0.00
Movie production method					
1	Live action	6,242	116,322,899,650	18,635,517	85.86
2	Animation/live action	58	7,851,551,219	135,371,573	5.80
3	Digital animation	86	7,414,920,351	86,220,004	5.47
4	Hand animation	103	3,372,425,321	32,741,993	2.49
5	Stop-motion animation	24	321,329,925	13,388,747	0.24
6	Rotoscoping	9	9,289,300	1,032,144	0.01
7	Multiple methods	5	1,021,618	204,324	0.00
Creative type					
1	Contemporary fiction	3,060	68,464,676,306	22,374,077	50.50
2	Kids fiction	250	14,048,858,940	56,195,436	10.36
3	Science fiction	297	12,834,206,223	43,212,816	9.47
4	Fantasy	335	12,489,562,626	37,282,276	9.21
5	Historical fiction	690	12,035,080,944	17,442,146	8.88
6	Dramatization	424	7,867,194,495	18,554,704	5.80
7	Super hero	43	5,910,527,800	137,454,135	4.36
8	Factual	721	1,604,816,540	2,225,820	1.18
9	Multiple creative types	10	9,451,971	945,197	0.01

SOURCE: *Nash Information Services*, http://www.the-numbers.com/market/.

In addition, the PWC report predicts that total U.S. cinema admissions will rise only slightly over the next five years to around 1.76 billion tickets sold. Ticket-price hikes nevertheless are expected to help fuel an approximate 5.4 percent total domestic box-office gain. [Source: Meredith Amdur, "Powerful Disc Drive—DVD Spending to Vastly Outweigh Box Office," *Variety.com*, June 28, 2004.]

Consumer spending. According to a study conducted by merchant bankers Veronis Suhler Stevenson, consumer spending on filmed entertainment in the United States will increase by more than 8 percent annually during the five-year period ending in 2009. That means overall consumer spending on filmed entertainment is expected to increase to $108 billion during that time period up from the $75 billion spent in 2003. That growth will apparently be fueled by new technologies that will give film distributors an increasing number of op-portunities to market movies. Such technologies extend the life of a movie and multiply its possible revenue streams and include digital film over the Internet, large library pay-per-view (iPods, computers, satellite), direct broadcasting, near video on demand and more.

The combination of the Internet, low-cost monthly subscriptions, and mail order allowing people to keep DVDs as long as they want is a winning formula across the United States, Europe and Australia. "DVD rentals in the USA overtook video and have stayed in the lead since last June when they hit the 28.2 million mark against 27.3 million video units," according to figures published by the Video Software Dealers' Association. With its strong movie culture, Europe has become a strong market, and Australia with its rental-friendly market is seen as the next new market for rentals. [Source: *DVD News Digest*, May 21, 2004].

It is no longer unusual for video sales to be twice or even three times the volume of theatrical sales. Moreover, DVD has already outstripped its VHS counterpart as the larger of the two components of home-video rentals. Neither is it unusual, even for a mediocre film, to recoup its costs solely from home-video revenues that may far outstrip a lackluster theatrical run. (Source: *VSDA—2003 Annual Report on the Home Entertainment Industry*.) With box-office revenues accounting for only 26 percent of a film's gross revenue, having a product that performs well in the ancillary markets is essential to a film's long-term success. [Source: "The Monster That Ate Hollywood," www.pbs.com, October 8, 2005].

DVD sales. As recently as 2007, the MPAA was reporting that DVD sales deliver more than 40 percent of a studio's international income. In addition, independent distributors have claimed gains in excess of 30 percent—due to an insatiable consumer appetite for rental but particularly sell-through DVD product. This phenomenal growth has been stimulating the marketplace in fundamental ways; providing novel business models, cost-effective exploitation of archive assets and even first-out distribution that circumvents the tricky theatrical sector. [Source: .www.mpaa.org].

On the other hand, home-video spending for 2008 ended slightly down for the year. The year's figures show DVD sales 4 percent to 5 percent behind 2007 levels, but Blu-ray sales jumped fourfold, making up a couple of percentage points of the DVD deficit. Overall disc sales ended 3 percent to 4 percent below 2007's $15.38 billion tally. Even so, total consumer spending on discs, rental included, topped $20 billion, as it has every year since 2002. However, that number is also down several percentage points from 2007's $22.9 billion. Rentals have been trending flat and Internet downloads are not yet a meaningful part of the equation. [Source: "Homevideo Biz Takes a Hit in '08," *Variety*, January 5, 2009].

Discount retail juggernaut Wal-Mart has been accounting for 33 percent of all DVD and VHS purchases, including used, in the United States, according to a survey of America's burgeoning population of DVD lovers. Based on data samples, market-research company NPD Group found that mass-market retailers as a whole are responsible for 42 percent of all VHS and DVD purchases. Best Buy is making inroads on Wal-Mart with 13 percent of all units sold, with rental shop Blockbuster and retailer Target claiming around 6 percent each. [Source: Meredith Amdur, "Wal-Mart Crowned DVD King," *Variety*, July 18, 2004.]

Brief history of DVD. From a historical perspective, the use of "DVDs did not take off quite as fast as some of the early predictions, but it has sold faster than the videotape, CD and laserdisc formats" (see table 6.5). "In fact, before the third anniversary of the availability of the DVD as of March 2000, the DVD had become the most successful consumer electronics entertainment product ever." As of the fall of 2003, 16 million DVD-video players had been shipped in the United States, adding to an existing installed base of 73.3 million. In addition, more than 27,000 titles in both DVD and video were available in the United States at the time and that number has certainly increased since. [Source: "DVD Frequently Asked Questions (and Answers)," *DVD Demystified*, http://dvddemystified.com/dvdfaq.html#1.9.]

Table 6.5.

Sales of DVD players in the United States from 1997 to 2004

Year	Sales (units)
1997[1]	315,136
1998	1,089,261
1999	4,019,389
2000	8,498,545
2001	12,706,584
2002	17,089,823
2003	21,994,389
2004	19,999,913

SOURCE: "CEA DVD Player Sales," *The Digital Bits*, http://www.thedigitalbits.com/articles/ cemadvdsales.html.

NOTE: 1997 is the year of introduction of DVD players.

"When DVD players became available in early 1997, Warner and Polygram were the only major movie studios to release titles. Additional titles were available from small publishers. The other studios gradually joined the DVD camp. Dreamworks was the last significant studio to announce full DVD support. Paramount, Fox and Dreamworks initially supported only Divx, but in the summer of 1998 they each announced support for open DVD." [Source: "DVD Frequently Asked Questions (and Answers)," *DVD Demystified*, http://dvddemystified.com/dvdfaq.html#1.9.]

"Eventually, DVD player sales exceeded VCR sales in 2001. DVD recorders [were] expected to hasten the death of VCRs once the price difference [was] small enough. DVDs have many advantages over tapes, such as no rewinding, quick access to any part of a recording and fundamentally lower technology cost for hardware and disc production. . . . By 2010, VHS may be as dead as vinyl records were in 2000." [Source: "DVD Frequently Asked Questions (and Answers)," *DVD Demystified*, http://dvddemystified.com/dvdfaq.html#1.9.]

As it turns out, VHS is now officially dead in the United States. In a November 14, 2006, article in *Variety*, with the headline "VHS, 30, Dies of Loneliness—The Home-Entertainment Format Lived a Fruitful Life," video retailers were reported to have announced that for their all-important fourth quarter, they would stop carrying the VHS format since "there was no longer shelf space." [Source: Diane Garrett, "VHS, 30, Dies of Loneliness: The Home-Entertainment Format Lived a Fruitful Life," *Variety.com*, November 14, 2006.]

Blu-ray high-definition. Blu-ray, also known as Blu-ray Disc (BD), is the name of a next-generation optical disc format. The format was developed to enable recording, rewriting and playback of high-definition video (HD), as well as storing large amounts of data. The format offers more than five times the storage capacity of traditional DVDs and can hold up to 25 gigabytes (GB) on a single-layer disc and 50GB on a dual-layer disc. [Source: "Blu-ray FAQ," *Blu-ray.com*, http://www.blu-ray.com/faq/#bluray.]

While this format is relatively new, it has made significant strides in the market. In 2007, nearly 9 million high-definition discs were sold, at a cost of $260 million (and that was during a format war that caused many consumers to assume a wait-and-see attitude). Market research firms suggest that by 2012, the installed base for Blu-ray players will range from 100 to 130 million households, a number approximately 20 percent higher than the current installed base of DVD players.

According to the *Hollywood Reporter*, $194 million was spent on Blu-ray discs in the first six months of 2008, which represents a 350 percent increase in sales compared to the combined sales of all high-definition discs sold in the similar months of 2007. The rate of Blu-ray disc sales is running well ahead of DVD sales for the same period in that format's formative years, which suggests the consumer's readiness to accept a new format that provides a better viewing experience. It is estimated that by 2012, Blu-ray disc sales will exceed that of DVDs, enjoying sales of $9.5 billion. [Source: Dan Ramer, "Blu-ray Disc Progress Report: Six Months after the Format War Victory," *DVDFile.com*, July 16, 2008.]

Distributor revenue streams. In comprehensive media studies, Paul Kagan Associates regularly presents estimated revenue forecasts for entertainment-media distributors. The data shows that some revenue streams are anticipated to grow in the years ahead, while others are anticipated to shrink (see table 6.6). The calculations are based on information from Paul Kagan Associates' reports *Mediacast 2008* and *Mediacast 2014*.

Table 6.6.

Estimated entertainment-media distributor revenue streams for 2008 and 2014

Revenue sources	2008 (millions $)	Revenue stream (%)	2014 (millions $)	Revenue stream (%)
Domestic (North America)				
Basic cable	2,532	4.42	4,316	5.91
Broadcast networks	988	1.72	375	0.51
Home video	13,836	24.14	15,961	21.87
Hotel/airlines/military/other	104	0.18	131	0.18
Merchandising/licensing	977	1.70	1,602	2.19
Pay television	1,742	3.04	3,227	4.42
PPV/DBS/VOD/DVOD	2,828	4.93	2,266	3.10
Syndicated television	268	0.47	227	0.19
Theatrical rentals	5,739	10.01	6,701	9.18
Total domestic	29,014	50.61	34,806	47.55
Foreign/international				
Home video	6,623	11.55	17,666	24.20
Merchandising/licensing	1,936	3.38	2,389	3.27
Network TV/syndication	4,223	7.31	4,637	6.35
Pay television	4,211	7.35	4,128	5.55
PPV/hotel/airline	3,054	5.33	906	1.24
Theatrical rentals	8,257	14.41	8,459	11.59
Total foreign/international	28,304	49.49	38,185	52.20
Total domestic and foreign/international	57,318	100.10	72,991	99.75

SOURCE: *Kagan's MediaCast 2008* and *Kagan's MediaCast 2014*, Paul Kagan Associates, Carmel, CA.

The Independent Film Industry

Independent film. An independent film, by definition, is any film financed by a source other than major studio/distributors, such as Paramount, Universal, Warner Bros., Sony, Disney and 20th Century Fox. While the Picture may eventually be distributed by a major studio, the cost of production and the final preparation of a ready-to-project master—the "Master Cost"—comes from other sources, independent of such studios.

Otherwise, the same processes apply to an independent film as they do to a studio film—development, preproduction, principal photography and postproduction. As with *XYZ Film*, a smaller production company usually raises money for one film at a time. Often, these independent production companies are owned or controlled by the creative people involved, such as a writer/director, writer/producer or actor/producer complemented by a financial partner or investment group.

By working outside the studio system, an independent producer is free from the homogeneity of a studio production and can exercise more control over the look and style of the film. Without the deep pockets of the studio to fall back on, a high degree of focused, budgetary vigilance and cost monitoring needs to be implemented. This means that independent producers must devote more time to their projects and plan their budgets more efficiently by giving greater attention to their lower-budgeted material. Unlike studios, the independents avoid the overhead costs of maintaining large administrative staffs. Consequently, independent films are generally produced for a fraction of the cost of studio-produced films.

Historically, approximately a third of the major-studio releases have been produced by independent producers. And typically there has been a higher ratio of financial success (i.e., overall revenue generated as compared to production cost) with indie-acquired products over in-house studio productions.

Independent films also benefit from broader opportunities and increased flexibility. This is of great significance in a film's distribution phase when it is possible to license the rights to the picture to separate distribution entities thereby maximizing its earning potential—keeping the revenue streams from domestic (U.S. and Canada) and international markets separate.

Of significance to potential investors is the consideration that independently financed pictures provide an opportunity for both the investors and the producers to share the revenues of a film, unlike pictures financed by a larger studio where significant allocations of overhead and other charges require substantial deductions from the film's revenue stream and thereby drastically reduce the potential for investor profit.

Growing importance of the independent-film industry. The growth and success of the independent film is a continuing phenomenon in the motion-picture industry. Somewhat cyclical in nature from year to year, the trend really took off in the late 1970s. The boom was fostered in part by Robert Redford's Sundance Film Festival and filmmakers like John Cassavetes and others, who proved, conclusively, that it was possible to make a feature film for far less money than the studios did. This trend grew through the 1980s and 1990s as major studios underwent a radical process of restructuring when expensive production facilities and staff, significant overhead expenses and runaway productions forced them to follow new business models, calling for fewer films but expecting higher grosses per film. As a consequence, smaller companies with lower-budgeted films were able to command a bigger share in the market. Currently, independent films are now a firmly established and permanent segment of the motion-picture industry.

The Independent Film and Television Association (IFTA, formerly the AFMA) reports international sales by its member companies for 2006 in excess of $3.1 billion. [Source: 2006 IFTA Membership International Sales Survey.] In addition, the production cost and marketing for major studio/distributor releases have continued to increase. In 2005, the average cost of producing and marketing a major studio/distributor motion picture was just below $100 million [Source: Gregg Kilday, "MPAA's "05 Scorecard: Box Office Slips, Costs Stabilize," *Holly-*

wood Reporter, March 10, 2006.] With this ridiculously high price tag on studio films, foreign-market distributors started scavenging film markets hoping to find a reasonably priced independent film that can attract audiences and make money. In 2005 alone, the American Film Market, the largest North American independently driven trade forum, saw a 15 percent growth rate in the number of participating distributors. [Source: Gregg Kilday, "AFM Books Record Number of Exhibitors," *Hollywood Reporter*, November 15, 2005.]

Moreover, studies show studio-produced and released films suffered a 6.5 percent box-office retreat in 2005 as the studios were forced to watch some of their frustrated mainstream audiences turn to smaller, more independently driven stories, like *Crash* and *Hustle and Flow* [Source: B. Chapin, "Box-Office Slump Has Theaters Reeling," *Times Herald*, 2005.] Some industry observers suggest that this is because the recent strategy of studios to produce remakes, sequels, and biopics have left audiences longing for something more original. This effect could have been foreshadowed with the extreme success of independent films in 2004, including the hit sleeper *Napoleon Dynamite* and the highest-grossing independent film of all time, *The Passion of Christ*, which grossed more than $370 million at the box office. [Source: "Title Search Engine," www.imdbpro.com, 2006.]

These changes in the marketplace in the United States and abroad have created an ongoing demand for new movies. And yet, despite this demand, the Producers have observed that the proportion of motion pictures produced and released by the major studios has declined in recent years. Based on periodic reports in the industry trade publications, this is due largely to increased studio overhead and Hollywood production costs, which have driven the budgets of studio films up to an average of approximately $60 million (without considering marketing costs). Independent films, conversely, have experienced a growth in both number and percentage of total films released. With budgets averaging a fraction of the major studios, independent producers have been able to turn out films that have successfully competed with the higher-cost Hollywood films while also offering the possibility of a higher rate of return. The majors have recognized there is profit potential in the marketing and exploitation of independent films. Not surprisingly, this has led to a significant consolidation, whereby most all studios now own or are affiliated with an independent or specialty distributor (e.g., Disney/ Miramax, Paramount/Paramount Classics; Sony/Sony Pictures Classics and Screen Gems, Warner Bros./New Line, Fine Line and Warner Classics, Universal/ Focus (formerly USA [October Films and Gramercy Pictures]). Traditionally, as much as 50 percent of major/studio releases are of independently produced films. Thus, there is an opportunity for the LLC is to produce a quality motion picture that will be acquired for distribution by a major studio/distributor or specialty distributor affiliate or finally by one or more independent distributors such as the companies of the Independent Film and Television Association.

Independent films benefit greatly from "buzz." Events have recently shown that independent films with good "buzz" (pre-release notices by reviewers, film-festival success and good public relations, positive word-of-mouth) may not only survive but ripen and flourish. Significant examples are the *Blair Witch Project* and *My Big Fat Greek Wedding.* Both pictures were released on a relatively small number of screens nationwide. As audience approval grew and friends and family were referred, the films began to enjoy wider and wider release in more and more theaters in more and more cities. NO ASSURANCES CAN BE PROVIDED, HOWEVER, THAT THE LLC'S FILM WILL ACHIEVE SIMILAR NOTORIETY.

Sundance Film Festival. The Sundance Film Festival (held in Park City, Utah, late January each year and often promoted as the foremost platform for American independent cinema) in 2009 received 3,661 feature film submissions total (1,905 from the United States and 1,756 international films). These numbers represent a slight increase from 2008's overall submissions (3,624), but there were fewer U.S. films this year. Of those, 118 feature-length films were selected including 91 world premieres, 16 North American premieres and 5 U.S. premieres representing 21 countries and 42 first-time filmmakers, including 28 in the noncompetition categories. [Source: "2009 Sundance Film Festival Adds World Premiere of the Winning Season to Line Up," *Elites TV,* December 2008, http://www.elitestv. com/pub/2008/Dec/EEN495bd0359e656.html.]

Based on the following summary, it appears that film buyers (i.e., distributors) spent at least an estimated $16.1 million acquiring rights at the 2009 Sundance Film Festival, however, that amount is down from the previous year's reported $27 million.

Anchor Bay Films paid $3.5 million for North American and Australian rights to the David Mackenzie–directed comedy *Spread*, starring Ashton Kutcher as a modern "kept man." Kutcher is a Hollywood Hills womanizer who meets his match in a local waitress. Anne Heche also stars. Kutcher, Peter Morgan and Jason Goldberg produced through their company Katalyst Films.

Sony Pictures Classics paid $3 million for North and Latin American rights to *An Education*, a coming-of-age story (also described as an upbeat romance) set in 1960s London. The script was based on a Lynn Barber memoir and was adapted by novelist Nick Hornby. Carey Mulligan stars as a sixteen-year old British schoolgirl who falls hard for a charming older man played by Peter Sarsgaard. Dominic Cooper and Alfred Molina also star.

Newly formed Senator Entertainment paid just less than $3 million for domestic distribution rights to *Brooklyn's Finest*, a violent cop drama (a dark story of police officers struggling with their own morality). DVD rights went to Sony Pictures. The film was directed by Antoine Fuqua. It cost a reported $20 million to produce and stars Ethan Hawke, Don Cheadle and Richard Gere. The distributor also made an $8 million to $10 million P&A commitment as part of the deal.

Lionsgate paid $2 million for North American and British rights to *Winning Season*, a story of an alcoholic (played by Sam Rockwell) coaching a girls' high school basketball team (also described as a femme-sports picture). The film was directed by James Strouse and also stars Emma Roberts. Plum Pictures and Gigi Films produced.

Sony Pictures Worldwide Acquisitions Group spent $2 million for North American rights for *Black Dynamite*, a comic spoof of 1970s exploitation movies (i.e., an action comedy).

Fox Searchlight purchased rights to another romance, *Adam*, starring Rose Byrne and Hugh Dancy as New Yorkers in life, for low-seven figures.

IFC bought rights to *In the Loop*, a British political farce for nearly $1 million. The film was directed by Armando Iannucci and produced by Kevin Loader and Adam Tandy. It follows a British government minister who inadvertently supports a war while on prime-time television. The film stars Tom Hollander, Peter Capaldi, James Gandolfini and Steve Coogan.

Magnolia Pictures acquired the rights to distribute *Humpday*, a comedy about two college buddies testing their friendship (i.e., straight men making a gay pornographic film). Magnolia only paid $100,000 for the film's domestic rights and plans to sell international rights. Magnolia also plans to introduce the film first through pay-per-view outlets and then release it theatrically in a dozen or so theaters.

IFC Films also acquired U.S. distribution rights to the tongue-in-cheek Nazi zombie scare story *Dead Snow*. The Norwegian horror picture is about medical-student coeds on a ski holiday who meet up with evil Nazi zombies. It was produced by Tomas Evjen, Ankhetil Omberg and Terje Stromstad.

Sony Pictures Classics will handle the domestic theatrical release of the sci-fi thriller *Moon*, which had its first public screening at the Sundance Film Festival this year. However, the film had been purchased before the festival run by the Sony Pictures Worldwide Acquisition Group. *Moon* features the voice of Kevin Spacey and stars Sam Rockwell as an astronaut who is assigned to a three-year mission to mine energy source Helium 3 on the moon.

New technologies and related revenue sources. There are continually new avenues of distribution and delivery technology. More TV channels are being created, and high-tech movie megaplexes are changing the landscape of the foreign-distribution marketplace, especially in France, Italy, Eastern Europe and Russia. In the domestic U.S. market, which started the trend, giant cineplexes or megaplexes with ten to twelve screens per complex have replaced the local single-screen or three-screen theaters.

A number of new technology-driven film delivery/distribution methods are expected to begin maturing during the "exhibition life" of *XYZ Film* and may become important additional revenue sources. Among them are:

Pay-per-view (PPV)
Direct Broadcast Satellite (DBS)
Near Video on Demand (NVOD)
Video on Demand (VOD)

The movie-piracy problem. A recent study of movie piracy indicates that online piracy (conducted by peer-to-peer networks) is costing the film business about $850 million per year in revenue. The study, released in January of 2005 by Informa Media Group, found that the estimated lost revenues stemming from digital piracy is about 25 percent of that for hard-copy piracy, which the group estimated to be around $3.5 billion for 2004. DVD piracy has been estimated at somewhere between $3 billion and $4 billion. The Informa "Film on the Internet" report is the first to attach a figure to the growing phenomenon of Internet piracy. According to the study, digital piracy is expected to nearly double to $1.7 billion by 2010, while hard-copy piracy is expected to grow less aggressively to $4.5 billion.

In the meantime, the MPAA has broadened its antipiracy campaign online with a second round of lawsuits directed towards alleged downloaders of pirated movies. The MPAA's member studios are also suing operators of indexing servers that help users locate and download pirated content.

The impact of Internet piracy is somewhat mixed, however. Some film-industry observers indicate that many of the films being downloaded are of such poor quality that they are less likely to influence someone's decision not to purchase the film through legitimate channels. In other words, the downloading of poor-quality films may actually be serving as an extended promotional trailer for the movie, creating an increased desire to see a better-quality version of the same film. On the other hand, the study also concludes that the biggest threat from piracy may be its tendency to generate bad buzz for a film, thereby discouraging people to see the film legitimately.

Even though the study agrees that piracy is a significant problem, the study also noted that if pirated movies were considered a part of the global film business in 2004, bootleg DVDs would have represented only 4.3 percent of revenue worldwide, while the illegal downloads from the Internet would have represented only 1.1 percent of worldwide revenue.

In the meantime, the report suggests that the legitimate online film business is still in its infancy, reporting that in 2004, Internet video-on-demand revenues from sites such as CinemaNow and Movielink totaled a mere $11.7 million. The report indicates that such revenues are expected to increase to nearly $1 billion in 2010. The study concludes that the time may be right to expand those businesses because of reducing price points, flexible business models and advancements in home networking. [Source: Ben Fritz, "Study: Web Piracy Costing Bix $850 mil—Informa's Report First to Attach Figure to Growing Practice," *Variety.com*, January 27, 2005.] NEITHER THE LLC OR ITS MEMBER-MANAGERS ARE AFFILIATED IN ANY WAY WITH THE PUBLISHERS OF THE INFORMATION REGARDING THE FILM INDUSTRY AS REPORTED ABOVE.

7. The Product or the Film Project

As with the other traditional headings for the major sections in a business plan, "The Product" is a bit too generic for a film-related business plan. The section may be more appropriately referred to as "The Film," or "The Films," "The Motion Pictures" or "Description of the Film Project," but something more specific than "The Product" and more directly related to the film industry seems preferable.

Scope of the project. It is possible that a filmmaker will set out to raise money from prospective investors to produce an educational film, an industrial film, a documentary, an infomercial, a television pilot, a video game, a live stage play or even a feature-length movie just for DVD release. It is up to the filmmaker to define the scope of the project. But it is also the filmmaker's responsibility to demonstrate to the prospective investors that the project can be commercial in that it can possibly make money for the investors. That's usually done through some sort of "box-office comparables" or "comparable earnings" research or other presentation relating to the commercial performances of similar projects released in the past (see "Box-office comparables" below). This chapter and most of the book are written based on the assumption that the project is a feature or documentary film being prepared for theatrical release, recognizing that even if the project does not get a theatrical release, it still may be exploited in other markets and media. If another type of project is the subject of the business plan, this information obviously needs to be modified to suit the specific need.

Some individuals seeking to raise financing from investors for a film or film-related business venture damage their own credibility by appearing to "take over the world." Their very first venture is so ambitious and out of sync with their backgrounds and anything else they've accomplished thus far in their lives that it becomes virtually impossible for them to raise the amount of funds they seek. Nobody believes they are going to be able to do what they are claiming, and even a well-written business plan is not going to solve that. Although it is not the place of a business-plan consultant to tell filmmakers and entrepreneurs that they cannot accomplish what they have set out to do, it is important that filmmakers and entrepreneurs be very realistic about their prospects. In most instances, if a filmmaker has never produced a feature film before, it is probably better to start with a single film project as opposed to seeking investor financing for an ambitious slate of films or a motion-picture franchise opportunity including merchandising and associated video game or a vertically integrated corporate conglomerate. It's great to think big, but looking at the proposed transaction from an investor's point of view, the investor doesn't want to be nervous or scared off because the filmmakers appears unrealistic. The scope of the project or business venture needs to appear doable to prospective investors and consistent with the filmmaker's background (or the combined backgrounds of the team assembled).

This section of the business plan sets out the scope of the project. Subcomponents of "The Project," when seeking to finance the costs of a single feature-film project, might include a synopsis of the script, chain-of-title information, production strategy, locations and logistics, cast, crew, preproduction, principal photography, postproduction, marketing, distribution, target audience and box-office comparables. Multiple projects or related ventures require additional descriptions.

Synopsis. If the business plan is being used to raise development funds, this subsection may be referred to as a "Description of the Story"—the story to be told through the script. If the business plan is being used to raise money for the production of a slate of films, the synopses for the projects to be included or for which the rights have been optioned may be included. Again, a filmmaker needs to be very accurate in describing the situation with respect to whether these projects will be available to include in the slate. In this situation, if there are other projects that have not yet been selected, the filmmaker will want to disclose the factors to be considered in choosing the projects (e.g., specific genres, anticipated MPAA ratings, level of violence, recognizable actors, based on novels and so forth).

Once again, based on the assumption that business plans are not typically being used to approach prospective investors currently working in the film industry (since a producer's package is usually more appropriate in such situations), it is not necessary to include a treatment or a full script bound with the business plan or included as an exhibit. Of course, if a legitimate prospective investor wants to read the entire script, a filmmaker may be obligated to make that available. A synopsis of the script that is a half to three-quarters of a page in length will typically be adequate for prospective investors from outside the industry.

Different writers take differing approaches when writing script synopses. Some track the action of the film all the way through and even disclose the ending (after all, the business plan will not be seen by too many people, certainly not people active in the film industry, and the investors presumably have a right to know).

Others take a more promotional approach and leave the readers hanging with regard to the eventual outcome. Part of their concern is theft of ideas, and it does occur. But it is probably safe to say that theft of ideas relating to films is more common within the industry than it is when dealing with prospective investors from outside the film industry and not involved in the industry. In other words, in the view of most long-time observers of this industry, theft of ideas is more likely to occur when a film-industry outsider is pitching ideas to a production executive or submitting a script to industry financing sources, as opposed to when a filmmaker is disclosing information about a film project through a business plan to prospective investors from outside the film industry. After all, industry insiders have the wherewithal to produce and distribute films, and they only need the new ideas.

Screenplay rights. After the synopsis or synopses, it adds credibility to the business plan to include a brief paragraph about the status of the underlying rights or copyrights associated with the project. A filmmaker will want to identify the screenwriter or screenwriters, when the script was registered with the U.S. Copyright Office and the registration number, the same information for registration with the Writers Guild West, if done, and then describe the plan with respect to assigning these rights to the production company, if not yet acquired and/or to the investment vehicle when formed. Note that for investors in a film to be able to take advantage of some of the available federal or state tax incentives, they will need to be equity owners of the investment vehicle that owns the copyrights to the script and film. So, it is important to see that these chain-of-title and rights ownership issues are properly handled and disclosed.

Because many film-school students are often being misled into thinking that registration with the Writers Guild provides just as much protection as copyright registration, here's a brief review of seven reasons why filmmakers should register their scripts and films with the U.S. Copyright Office:

1. Registration is typically required by errors-and-omissions insurance carriers, so if a filmmaker wants his or her production insured, the script will need to be registered with the U.S. Copyright Office.
2. If a filmmaker wants to use Screen Actors Guild (SAG) actors, SAG will require a copy of the U.S. Copyright Office registration and receipt for the filmmaker's script's registration.
3. Copyright registration is typically required by film distributors, so if a filmmaker wants his or her film distributed, he or she will have to register it with the U.S. Copyright Office.
4. Registration allows the copyright owner to record registration with the U.S. Customs Service for protection against the importation into the United States of infringing copies.

5. If a filmmaker wants to file an infringement lawsuit in court, registration with the U.S. Copyright Office is required for works of U.S. origin.

6. If registration occurs before or within five years of publication, courts start with the presumption that copyright is valid and all facts in the certificate are correct.

7. If copyright registration is made within three months after publication of the work or prior to an infringement of the work, statutory damages and attorney's fees will be available to the copyright owner in court actions. Otherwise, only an award of actual damages and profits is available to the copyright owner. This makes it easier to get the help of an attorney.

Production strategy. After setting out the script synopsis and a discussion of the legal status of the script rights, a filmmaker may want to provide some discussion relating to how he or she plans to produce the film (or development of the script as the case may be). If the funds are being raised on a mini-maxi (minimum-maximum) basis, the filmmaker will want to explain what the minimum proceeds will allow him or her to do from a production standpoint (e.g., shoot on high definition video) or what he or she may be able to do with the maximum amount of proceeds (e.g., shoot on 35 mm film). The filmmaker may also want to explain how the production of a film is organized (e.g., divided into the three phases of preproduction, principal photography and postproduction), along with a brief description regarding what the filmmaker expects to accomplish during each of those three phases.

Locations and logistics. Here the filmmaker will want to disclose how the locations for shooting will be selected, where he or she anticipates that the film will be shot on location (if that's the case), what the setting is for the film and what locations are being considered or have been selected.

Casting. This paragraph will disclose the filmmaker's plans for casting the movie and whether he or she will use a casting director and, if known, who. The filmmaker will also want to talk briefly about the level of actors (e.g., relative unknowns, recognizable, SAG and so forth). A filmmaker might even discuss the advantages and/or disadvantages of his or her approach to casting.

Crew. Another paragraph discussing the filmmaker's crew plans can be included here. A filmmaker will want to discuss where most of the crew will be coming from and include some of the films that have been produced in the area with similar local crews, along with any additional information regarding the crew that may be available. If some of the top-level crew members will be coming from Los Angeles, mention that.

Principal photography and postproduction. Then the filmmaker may want to set out a brief description of the anticipated time period for each of the production phases along with the tasks to be accomplished during that phase, possibly including the approximate budget percentage that will be expended during that time period.

Marketing and Distribution

This material may be treated as a subsection of "The Film Description" section or as a stand-alone section of the business plan. In either case, it should address the filmmaker's plans for marketing the completed film to prospective distributors as well as which distributors may be interested in such a motion picture, along with some discussion of how distributors operate. On the other hand, if functions of the distributor were included in the "Market Overview/State of the Industry," it would be inappropriate to repeat that information here.

Marketing to distributors. The films for which the development and/or production costs were paid for by a major studio/distributor or other distributor already have distribution arrangements in place since distribution was part of the financing deal. Thus, the in-house production/distribution deal and the production-financing/distribution deal include the distribution arrangements. Even the negative pick-up deal (and its other third-party-lender financing variations such as the split-rights deal or foreign presales) includes distribution; after all, without the distribution agreement and guarantee, the banks will not loan the production money.

For the independently produced feature films, however, particularly those developed and produced with investor funds, the producer is typically obligated to finalize distribution arrangements after the film is completed. There are essentially three ways in which this "marketing to distributors" activity occurs: produce DVDs of the movie and send them out to various distributors and their representatives, rent a theater or screening room in Los Angeles or New York and invite distributor representatives to a screening of the film and/or seek to enter the film in high-profile film festivals and markets that are commonly attended by distributor representatives. Such film festivals include Sundance, Toronto, Cannes, Telluride, Berlin, Venice, New York, Seattle, the Los Angeles Independent Film Festival and South by Southwest in Austin, along with the IFP Market and the American Film Market (AFM).[1]

Marketing to distributors requires some expenditure of funds beyond the normal production budget for a film. The activity is not a typical film-production budget item because it is not part of the production costs. Independent-film producers need to plan ahead and set aside some funds for this pursuit, otherwise, they may get caught with a marketable film but no funds available to pay for the costs associated with this specific form of marketing. So, it is important that the filmmaker include a line item in the "Estimated Use of Proceeds" subsection (but not in the film-production portion) that provides funding for this important activity.

As with most options in the film business, these choices relating to marketing to distributors have advantages and disadvantages. For example, many suggest that sending a DVD in to a distributor is the least-effective means of getting the distributor's attention because the DVD is likely to wind up in a stack of other unreviewed DVDs. This may actually depend on the relationship that exists between the distributor and the person who sent the DVD (or others associated with the producer) and on the filmmaker's follow-up efforts. It may also be difficult to get representatives of the distributors to attend screenings of new films in Los Angeles. On the other hand, the film festival circuit is competitive and typically more expensive than the other two options. So, there may not be any really good options, and they all cost money. Thus again, that line item in the "Estimated Use of Proceeds" section (not the film-production budget portion) should be set aside for this marketing-to-distributors activity.

This is also that critical period in the life of an independently produced motion picture when it may be beneficial to bring a producer's representative on board. This person's primary function is to help independent producers find a distributor for the film. A rather expansive description of all of the possible areas in which a producer's rep may help in moving a film project forward is found in entertainment attorney Harris E. Tulchin's article "Selling Your Movie: The Role of the Producer's Representative."[2]

Feature-film distribution. Many presentations relating to the phases in the life of a motion picture typically end after postproduction. But distribution is one of the most important phases in the life of a film. Authors of books to be read by film students or others interested in the film industry should not presume that all readers want to be producers. Some may want to be involved in distribution, and, of course, most producers of feature films want their films distributed.

A variety of distribution possibilities exist for an independently produced feature film. No two distribution deals are exactly alike, a statement that probably holds true for most businesses, and the motion-picture industry is no exception (see the examples in this chapter's section "Distribution Options" for a discussion of several possible scenarios for selling or licensing an independent film).

A brief list of some of the more active distributors to which independently produced feature films are typically marketed is below.[3] However, due to the recent deep recession in the general economy, which has impacted certain segments of the movie industry, some of these companies may be inactive.

Emerging Pictures	Paramount Classics
Fine Line Features Distribution	Picturehouse Films
Focus Features	Regent Releasing
Fox Searchlight Pictures	Seventh Art Releasing
Goldwyn/Roadside	Sony Pictures Classics

IFC Films

Independent Distribution Partnership (IDP)

Indican Pictures

Koch Lorber

Lions Gate Entertainment

Magnolia Pictures

MGM

Miramax Films

New Line Distribution

New Market Films

Strand Releasing

Submarine Entertainment

Technicolor

ThinkFilm

United Artists

Warner Independent

Weinstein Company, The

Wellspring Media

Wolfe Video

Zeitgeist

A fairly extensive list of currently active video and film distributors with online links appears at the VideoUniversity.com Web site.

Target Audience

Another subsection of a major business-plan section called "Description of the Film" or something similar may be a discussion and analysis of the film's target audience(s). It is reassuring to prospective investors to know that the producers of the proposed film have given some thought to the specific audience segments to which their film may appeal. So here the filmmaker wants to talk about the film's genre and the likely audience segment or segments to which that genre typically appeals. Further analysis may include other elements of the film such as whether the story is more apt to appeal to women versus men, what age audience, domestic/foreign appeal, for children, families, Christian audiences and/or gay/ lesbian and so forth. The filmmaker may also want to discuss the appeal of special effects or other specific characteristics of the planned movie. Some may prefer to use the subsection title "Demographics and Target Audience" for this discussion.

Box-office comparables. This is another one of those subsections relating to the specific film or films that requires some current research. Fortunately (and as noted earlier), many Web sites are devoted to providing some statistical information regarding the performances of feature films at the box office. Box-office information with results from more than fifty thousand movie screens in fourteen countries is online at Nielsen EDI.[4] The company's products include custom research. BOFFO (Box Office Flash Figures Online) is a Web-based system that offers real-time film performance on a national, regional, local or theater level; Filmsource is an online historical database with information on a film or filmmaker's history, present and future; Overnight Theatrical Box Office Reporting provides theater-by-theater box-office results as well as summaries and rankings of daily film performances at a national level; the Release Schedule is an online calendar for current and advance release information and historical performance data; School Holiday Calendar's software combines school-district holiday data with enrollment information on more than thirty million students. This calendar reports on the percentage and number of students on vacation every day of the year at the national, market, state, county and district levels; and Theatre Atlas plots theatre locations on street-level maps and indexes the listings with performance and profile data.

Worldwide box office analysis of current and past productions with a database of more than ninety thousand films is available through Show Biz Data, whose Data Distribution Guide also offers analysis of all U.S. and foreign distributors. The Show Biz Data Web site includes information relating to industry news, box office, development and production, along with job listings and a calendar.[5]

Another supplier of box-office information is the Box Office Report. This online service offers box-office forecasts, box-office previews, theatrical-release dates, DVD/video–release dates, weekend-by-weekend box-office profiles, weekend estimates, weekend updates, final domestic projections, weekend top-twenty and box-office archives, discussion forums for actors and directors, lists of favorite movies, top domestic films, top worldwide films, top-grossing franchises, highest-production costs, largest openings, second- and third-largest weekends, quickest films to hit $100 million and $200 million, list of top-grossing films by distributor, links to movie trailers and other movie links.[6]

Other Web sites now offering some level of box-office information include:

@N-Zone	The HSJ
About.Com	*Los Angeles Times*
Asian Box Office	Lowe's Cineplex Entertainment
Baseline	Lumiere
Box Office Mojo	Movie Marshall
Box Office Prophets	Movie Times
Box Office Statistics	Movie Web
Box-Office Grosses	Movies Excite
Box-Office Guru	Mr. Showbiz
CIVILIAN Capital	The Numbers
Craig's Box-Office Database	ShowBizData
Entertainment Data, Inc.	The Sky is Falling
Entertainment Industry Online	The Trades
Exhibitor Relations Co.	*Variety.com*
The Hollywood Reporter	The Weekend Warrior
The Hot Button	World of KJ
Lee's Movie Info	WorldwideBoxOffice.com

Some business-plan consultants want to treat the box-office comparables as if it were part of the financial projections, but the two reports are distinctly different. Box-office comparables provide historical information that has been reported regarding the box-office performances of similar films (i.e., similar to the film the filmmaker is trying to produce). The similarity of the films selected is based primarily on the genre and level of budget. The financial projections, on the other hand, are peering into the future and attempting to make reasonable projections as to the possible financial results of an investment in the venture, based on certain stated assumptions. Because of this difference, the box-office comparables ought to be included in the business-plan section dealing with the film, and the financial projections ought to be incorporated separately, most likely as an exhibit to the business plan. Another reason this works well is that since the person primarily responsible for preparing the financial projections may be someone different than the person primarily responsible for preparing the main body of the business plan, it is easier to insert the financial projections as an exhibit to the business plan. There is nothing wrong, however, with referring to the box-office comparables in the assumptions section of the financial projections, pointing out that the domestic or worldwide box-office-gross assumption used in preparing the "good performance" column of the financial projections, for example, was actually based on the average provided by the box-office comparables appearing in the main body of the business plan (citing the page number where the box-office comparables appear).

Thus, these two sections are not the same, but there is a relationship between the two. A reasonable average of the box-office comparables for similar films may serve as an assumption for the projected box-office-gross calculations in the financial projections. So, if the filmmaker has been fair in selecting which films to include in the box-office comparables and maybe even for averaging purposes thrown out the highest and lowest earners, the filmmaker's average box-office-performance figure may then become the assumed box-office gross for use in the "good performance" column of the financial projections. Such an assumption would have to be considered "reasonable," one of the standards for the written assumptions that accompany the financial projections and upon which the financial projections are based (see chapter 10).

Although some filmmakers may want to provide more columns of performance-related information for similar films, the following headings are adequate:

Film title
Year of release
Distributor
Estimated budget
Domestic box-office gross

It is not necessary to include the exact day of release. That's too much information. Giving the year of release only is enough. The filmmaker also may want to order the films chronologically. It is good practice to include the word "estimated" before "budget" because the filmmaker is clearly relying on secondary sources, which in the film industry are not always exact. He or she is simply reporting in good faith the best information that is available. It is also important to be precise in the column heading as to whether the box-office-gross information is for the domestic marketplace, the international marketplace or worldwide. To confuse those would be very misleading and could significantly throw off the financial projections. So, in other words, do not just use "Box Office Gross" as the heading for this column, since readers won't know whether the numbers are for domestic, international or worldwide box-office performances.

As noted, some filmmakers want to also include columns for the name of the production company, international box office, worldwide box office, DVD results and even some profit ratio. However, as a practical matter, there may not be enough horizontal space on the page for additional columns of unneeded information. This section, after all, is typically entitled "Box Office Comparables"; thus anything beyond the box-office-performance numbers goes beyond the scope of the heading. Further, all that is needed to serve as a reasonable assumption for the financial projections to be prepared later is that average domestic-box-office-gross number. After all, the other reasonable assumptions to be used in calculating the financial projections can be drawn from the percentages for each revenue stream offered by Paul Kagan Associates' research cited in chapter 6 (as well as in chapter 10) or from other published reports relating to distributor revenue streams.

The filmmaker may want to provide several levels of box-office comparables. Research may turn up a small number of films, for example, that are very similar to the filmmaker's with respect to genre and budget, but that research may also find a lot of other films that are either similar with respect to genre but not in the same budget range or vice versa. Thus, the filmmaker may want to list each grouping separately in the box-office-comparables subsection, so that readers will understand the filmmaker's use of such film box-office performances is reasonable and that the filmmaker is being upfront with them about which ones are similar and why. For purposes of taking an average that can later be used as an assumption for the financial projections, the filmmaker will have to decide which to include in the averaging process and provide an explanation for his or her choices. It is usually preferable to take a more conservative approach in such matters.

In order to protect the credibility of the box-office comparables, source citations ought to be included at the bottom of the chart, so that prospective investors can be assured that the numbers were not created out of whole cloth.

Sample "Description of the Film Project"
Script Synopsis—XYZ Film

In the 1980s, a disciplined Central American boxer achieved his dream of moving to the United States. He got married, opened up a small auto shop and proudly raised his family. Twenty years later, his children have grown into young adults. His angelic daughter is a medical student at a private university, but his son, DIEGO, becomes an enforcer for a local mixed-martial-arts fight promoter who deals illegal high-performance drugs to athletes. Diego ends up convicted of assault and battery and spends three years in prison.

Our film begins when Diego is being released form prison on parole. An undercover agent, BOB ANDERSON, pretends to be Diego's probation officer. He manipulates Diego, forcing him to get back involved with mixed martial arts. Bob uses Diego to gather information about what he believes is a giant biotech conspiracy.

Diego visits his father's auto shop hoping to reconcile his relationship. Before they even speak, his father gets shot in the head by one of Diego's adversaries. Due to the fact that Diego's father was the sole provider for his family, Diego is forced to take on the responsibility of providing for his mother, younger sister and his illegitimate son . . . a task for which he is not equipped. He becomes highly motivated and decides to follow Bob's lead for his own purpose—to win the purse at the mixed-martial-arts tournament called the Red Canvas and save his family from financial ruin.

Through his journey, he discovers his father's inspiring boxing legacy. His family rallies behind him as he becomes disciplined and focused on righting his past mistakes and pressing toward the goal of supporting his family. He learns the value of humility and the power of mentorship from his father's ex-boxing coach, a quirky martial-arts-master named BANG. In the end, Diego saves his father's business, reconciles with his family, becomes a championship fighter and evolves into a productive American hero.

Screenplay rights. The Screenplay for *XYZ Film* was written by Tim Burnson, Peter Knarley and J. T. Nixon. The Screenplay was registered with the U.S. Copyright Office on March 30, 2008 (PAU 3–745–112). Upon funding of the Offering, certain movie and related rights to the Script will be transferred from the owners to the LLC. A Short Form Assignment similar to the example provided at Exhibit "C" will be recorded in the U.S. Copyright Office as evidence of the transfer of rights.

Production strategy. The Minimum of Investor funds, plus creative Deferments, if any, will allow the LLC to acquire rights to the Script, produce the Film and market it to film festivals and prospective distributors. The Maximum plus Deferments, if any, will allow the LLC to acquire the rights to the Script, to use more advanced technology, attract better-known actors, improve resources (such as locations, set dressings, music, and the like) and market the film more aggressively. The production of *XYZ Film* will be divided into three main phases: preproduction, principal photography and postproduction. Preparation for filming will involve selecting each member of the cast and crew, scheduling each day of production, constructing sets and costumes and negotiating arrangements with suppliers of equipment and facilities.

Locations and logistics. Prior to the commencement of preproduction, the Film's director, Producers and cinematographer will scout locations, precast and secure deals with postproduction entities, equipment rental houses and studio/ sound stages, if necessary. The setting for the Picture is contemporary small-town rural America. However, it is the intention of the director and Producers that *XYZ Film* will be shot on locations in and around Lansing and Detroit, Michigan.

Casting. While casting is important to the success of a motion picture and the Producers intend to attach recognizable talent for multiple roles, *XYZ Film* is not a "star dependent" movie. The Producers intend to cast Screen Actors Guild (SAG) talent for the Movie. As has been demonstrated in the past with other successful independent films, casting talented but relative unknowns can ultimately be a positive selling point in a marketplace saturated with overexposed and overhyped stars. Without preconceived expectations, critics, distributors, film-festival goers and ultimately audiences around the world, can "discover" the intrigue of a picture, like *XYZ Film*, and make it their own. Their subsequent enthusiasm and "word of mouth" may then become a major, cost-effective tool used to market and promote the movie.

Crew. The majority of below-the-line crew for *XYZ Film* will be selected from the capable pool of Michigan film crews from the Greater Detroit area, augmented by key personnel from Hollywood.

Principal photography and postproduction. Filming of *XYZ Film* is tentatively scheduled to begin approximately two months after the close of the segregated, interest-bearing account that will hold Investor funds during the period in which funds are being raised; the filming will last for approximately five (5) six-day weeks. After principal photography is completed, the postproduction phase will take place in Los Angeles. During this phase, the director and Producers will supervise the final-editing process, build up the sound track, score the Film, add titles and optical effects and ultimately produce a digital master from which a distributor can strike release prints.

PRODUCTION SCHEDULE AND TIMETABLE

The following is the preliminary schedule of events and expenditures for *XYZ Film:*

Preproduction. 24 weeks (currently underway)

Active preproduction commences with the successful funding of the project. Thereupon, a skeletal staff of key personnel will begin the preparations for the production. The purpose is to organize and prepare for principal photography. Approximately 10 percent of the budget is used during preproduction.

To be accomplished:
Complete casting
Finalize script changes
Crew allocation
Lock-in production schedule
Lock-in all locations
Allocation of equipment, props, wardrobe
Cast rehearsals
Begin initial publicity
License/compose and record onscreen music

Principal Photography/Production. 5 weeks
Production or principal photography begins when shooting actually starts. At this point, the entire crew is employed on the film, and the cast is traveling or working according to need. Approximately 70 percent of the budget is used during production.

To be accomplished:
Meet each day's production needs, in terms of equipment, actors, crew, lodging, food, supplies, locations, props, effects, construction, set dressing, and the like.
Transfer of High Definition files
Begin postproduction editing
Cut the trailer to initiate industry attention

Postproduction. 18 weeks
Postproduction commences upon the completion of principal photography. Production personnel are released and equipment is turned in. During Postproduction, the director supervises the editor's "cutting" of the Film, and it is readied for presentation and distribution.

To be accomplished:
Director supervises editing of the Film with editor
Edit sound
Creation and integration of visual and sound effects
Compose, record and edit score
Shoot any required pickup shoots, or reshoots
Rerecord any necessary dialogue
Creation of main and end titles
Spot music and sound effects
Mix music, sound effects and dialogue
Color time (color correct) the film

Create digital master

Screen *XYZ Film* for distributors

MARKETING AND DISTRIBUTION

The Producers of *XYZ Film* will begin to seek distribution during preproduction since it is never too early to create "buzz" in the worldwide film-market communities. During production, the Producers plan to design a Web site and cut a trailer that can be sent to possible national and international distributors and other media companies to continue to garner interest.

The Producers believe that the key to selling an independent film is to do so when its value is at its greatest. Typically holding off until after the project is completed is preferred, at which time the Film has hopefully captured the attention of choice distributors through the previously mentioned "buzz," by timely and appropriate industry screenings and by exploiting favorable reviews at high-profile festivals such as the American Film Market, Berlin, Cannes, Milan, Sundance and Toronto.

The goal of the LLC's marketing strategy is to promote the Film to potential distributors both directly and through the film-festival circuit in order to sell the distribution rights outright. The LLC's first priority is to secure a single worldwide or major-market distributor. In lieu of this approach, the LLC will then consider market-by-market sales.

Sales strategy. The Producers' goal throughout all phases of the production will be to produce a top-quality motion picture competitive with the best in the industry while maintaining strict cost control. Ultimately, the Producers intend to make *XYZ Film* known to all distributors with the capability to market the Film with the specialized attention and care necessary to maximize its potential revenues. In order to achieve this, the Producers intend to do one or more of the following:

- establish and maintain an ongoing dialogue with potential distributors throughout the Film's production and postproduction period
- possibly employ the services of a producer's representative if the Member/Managers feel such a producer's rep can negotiate more advantageous deals with a distributor for the domestic, foreign and media markets
- offer private screenings of the finished film to distributors
- seek to enter *XYZ Film* in high-profile film festivals like Berlin, Cannes, Sundance, Toronto, and Venice, in order to generate positive word-of-mouth and critical "buzz"
- create a Web site for *XYZ Film* where the LLC can engage in preliminary promotional activities to build awareness for the Film, targeting both the trade and potential viewers (e.g., run trailers, interviews with

actors, show behind-the-scenes footage, and/or hold contests geared to the Film's demographic)

- actively create industry "buzz" once accepted to a major festival. The Producers intend to send out press kits with publicity stills, actor head-shots, a synopsis, biographies of key persons, "making-of" blurbs, and possibly a trailer, teaser or poster to selected distributors seeking to make them aware of the Film's festival screenings. The Producers will also submit press kits to the local media and seek positive reviews from such papers. The intention is to create "buzz" about the Film before the festival begins in an attempt to sell out the festival screening and have as many distributors as possible in the theater. The Producers believe that having a screening at a festival sometimes is not enough, that it is the quality of the screening that counts.

In addition to the marketing campaign that a distributor (if any) will set into motion, the Producers of *XYZ Film* also intend to engage in independent "guerilla" marketing. After this Private Placement Offering is completed, the Producers will begin to publicize the film online as well as through various local Los Angeles–area publications including www.Tailslate.net, *Independent Film Magazine, Filmmaker Magazine, MovieMaker Magazine, Hollywood Reporter, VideoMaker Magazine* and *Variety*.

Given the content and the anticipated execution of *XYZ Film*, the Producers feel the Film will attract attention from various distributors for a number of reasons, including:

1. Genre. The Producers of *XYZ Film* intend for the project to fall within the comedic family film genre, with touches of contemporary fantasy, thus providing wide appeal wrapped into one specialty independent picture. They believe that this film type enjoys worldwide distribution demand and according to the statistics of the American Film Market, these genres have consistently combined to account for a significant percentage of market share. The Producers believe that comedic family films are especially appealing to distributors because this genre has a track record of performing well in the ancillary markets, like DVD and pay cable. With box-office revenues accounting for a significant percentage of film gross revenues when given a theatrical release, having a product that performs well in the ancillary markets is essential to a film's long-term success, something distributors keep in mind when searching for films to acquire.

2. Style. The independent market welcomes unconventional story elements like numerous main characters and unique aesthetics now more than ever. Even mainstream audiences have found themselves leaning to stories that challenge them on a structural level, and the Producers believe that is why TV, which has a reputation for taking the safe route, can have a show like *Lost* top the Nielson ratings [Source: "Nielsen Ratings Report," *Variety*, October, 2005]. The Producers believe that *XYZ Film* uses many stylistic elements that are now considered hip and marketable to distribution companies.

3. *Attractive to talent.* Specific marketable actors are being pursued for *XYZ Film*. With the level of characterized internal conflict in *XYZ Film* of the sort that tends to garner award attention, the Producers believe they will attract at least one recognizable name actor to perform in the movie, something that distribution companies typically consider important when first considering the acquisition of a film. The Producers believe that attaching such a recognizable name actor could be an asset in the Film's ability to attract distribution.

4. *MPAA rating.* With an MPAA rating of PG, the Producers believe *XYZ Film* will be appropriate for a universal, and thus potentially much larger, audience. The Film will not contain gratuitous sex or violence. The Producers represent that all content in the Film will be handled in a tasteful manner.

5. *Festival appeal.* The Producers believe that film festivals provide a useful gateway to distributors. They also believe that festivals and distributors respond well to stories that have quirky subject matter, an eclectic mix of unique characters and originality. Sundance's Web site states they are "dedicated year-round to the development of artists of independent vision and to the exhibition of their new work" [Source: "About Sundance Institute," www.sundance.org, 2005]. The Toronto Film Festival as well as Cannes, the biggest festivals in the world, have similar mission statements. The Producers believe that *XYZ Film* utilizes an artistically distinct style of storytelling in addressing contemporary issues that heralds back to classical filmmaking traditions and that this combination of elements are likely to result in a favorable festival reception.

6. *Low cost.* Many production entities and distributors consider the low-budget category of films to be in the $5 to $10 million range [Source: "From Reel to Deal," Dov Simens, 2003]. With the story limited to just a few locations and the Producers' plans to shoot in cost-effective locations, the Producers have been able to dramatically pare the budget. Furthermore, the Producers will seek to negotiate contributions of certain goods and services to be used in the production of the Film in exchange for a participation in the original member/manager's share of the LLC's Distributable Cash. The Producers believe that such arrangements will enable them to engage in and attract attention from various distributors because of the relatively low asking price for a product that they expect will be able to compete with films produced on studio-inflated budgets.

On the other hand, no assurances can be provided that the Producers will be able to enter into any arrangement with any distribution company for the Film or that the Film will be accepted into any film festivals. In general, the availability of film-release slots on distributors' schedules for so-called acquisitions are limited. However, once the Film has been completed, assuming it is a quality film, there is less risk for a distributor than with a film that has been presold based on the package alone. Thus, again assuming the Film is a quality motion picture, an independent producer may be able to negotiate more favorable terms by waiting to make a distribution deal after the film has been completed.

Distribution Options

As noted earlier, no two distribution deals are exactly alike, a statement that holds true for any business, and the motion-picture industry is no exception. Following are several possible scenarios for selling an independent film.

Studio distribution. It is possible that an independently produced feature film like *XYZ Film* could be acquired for distribution by a major studio/distributor. All marketing and distribution decisions are then made in-house at the studio, which sends out promotional and advertising materials, arranges for screenings of the films and makes deals with domestic and foreign distributors. For the foreign markets, studios have offices around the world either singly or with other studios to distribute their films in other countries. The studio acquires (or licenses) the copyright, which it licenses to the foreign distributor for a specific length of time. Once the studio receives its share of the box-office grosses from the exhibitors, the distribution arm will charge a distribution fee that can range from 30 percent to 40 percent. The studio then takes the entire fixed cost of the distribution division and applies a portion of it to each film (its so-called overhead), often around 12 percent of the distributor's gross receipts. They also recoup their costs of advertising and for prints and other distribution expenses. Although these deductions from the Film's revenue stream may seem excessive, there are some advantages to studio distribution. The studios have the ability to put three thousand prints of one film in circulation on opening weekend. Their own channels of distribution are manifold. The studios have the financial resources to inundate television and the press with ads, and they have significant clout in scheduling appearances for producers, directors and actors on early-morning and late-night national interview shows.

Studio advance, buy-out or guarantee. Some independent films acquired by studios or distribution companies receive an advance or guarantee against future proceeds. *Shine* was reported by the *Los Angeles Times* (March 4, 1997) to have a negative cost of $4.5 million (the negative cost of a film is defined as the total of all the various costs, charges and expenses incurred in the acquisition and production of a motion picture, in all its aspects prior to release, that is, to produce the final negative). The film reportedly received $10 million as domestic and international advances. According to the *Hollywood Reporter* (November 14, 1996), *Slingblade* had a negative cost of $1 million and was acquired by Miramax with a $10 million guarantee. *Spitfire Grill* reportedly had a negative cost of $6.1 million and was acquired by Castle Rock for a $10 million advance. Miramax is reported to have paid $5 million for *Swingers*, a film with a reported negative cost of $2 million (Levison, *Filmmakers and Financing*). In 2002, the indie film *Better Luck Tomorrow*, reportedly produced for a mere $150,000 was acquired for a theatrical release with a $1,000,000 advance from MTV Films. More-recent distributor advance numbers have declined (see the annual Sundance Film Festival summary reports below). In addition, the vast majority of independently produced feature films are not picked up for distribution by a major studio/distributor (or subsidiary), thus no such studio advances, buy-outs or guarantees may occur. NO ASSURANCES CAN BE PROVIDED THAT THE RIGHTS TO DISTRIBUTE THE LLC'S FILM IN ANY MARKET OR MEDIA WILL BE ACQUIRED BY ANY DISTRIBUTOR.

Independent distribution. Independent distribution is similar to studio distribution, but independent companies typically release fewer movies each year (per distributor); therefore they are presumed to be able to spend more time on providing individual attention to a motion picture's release. They also have expertise in marketing films that are smaller in scale with less "marquee" value and the patience to not give up on a film as quickly as some of the major studio/distributors. The fee an independent-distribution company takes will depend largely on its involvement in the film, how large a risk it is taking and how badly it wants to distribute the film. The amount of risk is primarily related to the amount of money the distribution company pays out of its pocket. The more up-front expenses it has to assume, the greater the percentage of incoming revenues it will seek. Its distribution fees apply only to the revenues generated by the distributor's own agreement (i.e., if it is not the foreign distributor, it does not share in the foreign profits). When an independent distributor acts in the same way a studio would (i.e., advance all the up-front costs or prints and advertising), the distribution deal often provides for a 50/50 split of net profits between the producer and distributor. But unlike a studio, which typically deducts any distribution costs off the top or takes its 30 percent to 40 percent of the domestic gross box-office rentals and deducts the distribution expenses from the producers' share, an independent distributor may split the distribution expenses equally between itself and the producers.

Foreign sales. It is common for a producer to make distribution deals with separate distributors for domestic and foreign releases. In order to reach a foreign distributor, a sales agent is usually employed. A sales agent is more likely to secure a foreign distribution for a film if there is already a deal for domestic theatrical release already in place, but, as discussed in the Distribution section, a domestic theatrical release is not necessarily an indicator of a film's eventual success overseas. Sales in foreign countries center around the big three international markets: the American Film Market held in Santa Monica, California, in November, The MIF (Marche International du Film) held in Cannes, France, concurrently with the Cannes International Film Festival and MIFED (Mercato Internazionale Filme e

Documentario) held in Milan, Italy, in October. Distributors come to these markets from around the world to view films. Sales to foreign distributors usually involve an advance against a percentage from the territory for which the sale is made.

Table 7.1 lists the top-eleven foreign territories in terms of overall theatrical sales, video sales and TV sales for the independent-distribution entities that make up the Independent Film and Television Alliance. The territories are ranked by company revenues.

Table 7.1.
Top eleven foreign territories in overall theatrical, video and TV sales for IFTA, 2006

Rank	Territory	Sales ($)	Percentage of sales (%)
1	Germany (including Austria)	475,273,135	14.96
2	U.K. (including Ireland)	359,291,480	11.31
3	France (including French Belgium)	309,433,304	9.75
4	Japan	292,589,775	9.21
5	Spain	231,335,598	7.28
6	Italy	188,283,278	5.93
7	Brazil	149,966,061	4.72
8	Australia/New Zealand	142,775,849	4.50
9	Russia/former USSR	127,716,600	4.02
10	Benelux[1]	118,745,126	3.74
11	Scandinavia	102,679,948	3.23
	Total foreign sales		78.65

SOURCES: *Independent Film and Television Alliance* (IFTA), 2007, http://www.ifta-online.org/ Publications/Default.aspx.

NOTE: 1. Benelux is an economic union in Western Europe comprising Belgium, Luxembourg and the Netherlands.

Rent-a-distributor. Somewhere between turning the film over to a distributor and four-walling (producers rent a theater and its staff) falls a practice known as rent-a-distributor. The producer puts up the money for all film prints and advertising and rents a distributor's in-place distribution-and-collection system. The producer usually pays 12.5 percent to 17.5 percent of the gross film rentals (the box-office receipts received by the distributor), which is far less than a producer gives up when a distributor risks money in advances and the cost of an advertising campaign. The producer retains more control over the marketing and advertising of a campaign. The distribution company provides its internal system, which includes in-house bookers to book the film into the theaters, a bookkeeping system to keep track of the money and follow up on receivables. A major studio will typically get a much-faster response from a theater chain on an overdue account than a single producer. The "rented" distributor will often take care of preparing and shipping publicity material and film prints although the producer will typically cover the cost.

Self-distribution. Although not an easy task, if all other efforts to obtain distribution from established distributors fail, the Producers reserve the right to pursue self-distribution opportunities. Four-walling, a form of self-distribution, is not common, but it is an alternative way to distribute an independent film and can be profitable. A producer rents a theater, usually for a flat weekly fee. The rental fee includes the theater staff (manager, projectionist, ticket and concession-counter salespeople). The entire box-office income is paid to the producer. The producer is also responsible for the cost of the print as well as any advertising.

Markets. There are multiple markets and media from which a producer of a completed motion picture can seek to generate revenue: domestic and foreign theatrical, the home-video market, foreign and domestic pay, cable and syndicated television, network television, the expanding Internet/broadband audience, as well as ancillary distribution to airlines, hotels, military services, educational institutions and other nontheatrical venues. Revenue may also be derived from rights such as the creation of books, novelization of the screenplay, published music, soundtrack albums and merchandise. The LLC will attempt to generate revenues from all ancillary rights held by the LLC (for a more detailed description of each market, see "Motion-Picture-Industry Overview" in chapter 8).

These markets and media may be handled by a single distributor, or the Producers may elect to seek separate distributors who specialize in various markets and media. In the event that sufficient funding is raised, the Producers may also seek to arrange for a rent-a-distributor deal or even engage in self-distribution. In situations other than self-distribution, the Producers plan to approach such prospective distributors with a completed or nearly completed film, thus potentially maximizing the LLC's bargaining position with respect to negotiating the terms of distribution arrangements.

The terms of agreements between feature-film producers and distributors vary widely depending on the perceived potential of a film and the relative bargaining strength of the parties. Customarily, a distributor will advance funds to the production company for the right to distribute its film and will agree to expend a minimum amount for prints and advertising. An advance or guarantee may range from a token fee to an amount in excess of the entire production cost. The distributor ordinarily requires that all its advances and expenses be recouped before percentage-participation monies are returned to the production company. The advertising costs plus the costs of publicity, print purchases, shipping, accounting and collecting are customarily deducted, along with a distribution fee, by the film distributor from gross film rentals. For a film such as *XYZ Film*, the costs incurred by a distributor to market and promote the film may be equal to or often exceed the cost of production.

Theatrical release strategy. In order to generate the highest-possible box-office gross in the first weekend, big-budget studio pictures usually rely on a blitzkrieg release strategy, with massive advertising and media spending, and often a thousand or more prints of a film in circulation. Independent or specialty films usually employ a much-different model. Primary among these is the platform release, whereby a film is released slowly, with a limited number of prints, in a limited number of cities, in order to build critical acclaim and word-of-mouth. As the film finds its audience base, the scope of distribution gradually expands, adding cities and theaters to meet demand. This method is the most common for specialty theatrical film distribution and the one the Producers expect will most likely be employed for a film like *XYZ Film*. If the Film successfully obtains a distributor, the Producers will make every effort to work together with the distributor to devise the optimal-release pattern within all applicable constraints.

Because it may be necessary for an "indie" to make separate distribution deals for international territories, these territories may see sequential distribution releases, which may take place over a twelve-month period following the Film's domestic theatrical release.

Domestic theatrical distribution. Assuming the Minimum is achieved for the Offering and the Producers complete the Film, the Producers plan to hold onto all distribution rights until the Picture is completed. The LLC will most likely license domestic rights to an independent or studio-affiliated specialty distributor, but if the opportunity arises, the LLC will also consider major studio/distributors. If the LLC is able to select among multiple proposals for domestic-distribution arrangements, its management will consider numerous factors, including amount of advance, if any, the distributor's reputation, the distributor's enthusiasm for the Picture, the distributor's proposed marketing campaign, print and ad commitments and the distributor's willingness to allow the Producers to contribute to the formation of the marketing campaign. In the unlikely event that the LLC has the opportunity (or is required by circumstances) to parcel out rights in domestic media to multiple distributors, the LLC will seek to maximize the value of each right in the Film. The most likely scenario for this occurrence would be if the LLC was not able to secure a theatrical release for the Picture. In such event, the LLC might still have the opportunity to license video, television and other U.S. or foreign rights to separate distributors.

Internet and broadband access. In addition to the above-mentioned ancillary markets is an exciting new distribution model emerging within the context of filmed entertainment. Technological advances such as digital satellite transmission, cable modems and DSL handheld cellular devices, all geared to high-speed broadband Internet access, are providing another potential avenue for audiences around the world to view their entertainment product. Already, numerous well-financed online entities are actively distributing—"net-casting"—short-form, archived and streaming media-entertainment content over the Web.

By the time *XYZ Film* is completed, the Producers anticipate several "net-casters" will have the ability to release and distribute a theatrical quality, full-length motion picture over the Internet, on a global basis, essentially bypassing traditional distributors and their high costs and fee structures. The advantages are clear: the potential for global distribution and worldwide release, content immediately available for repeated viewings, no print costs, no shipping costs and instantly verifiable next-day collections—plus the ability to better target the Film's potential audience, as well as run trailers and online promotion, twenty-four hours a day, seven days a week, without costly network television media buys. The challenge is to get people to the site and motivate them to pay for the viewing.

Intense competition among emerging companies to establish a recognizable brand in the Internet entertainment space will likely lead to increased distribution opportunities and a new class of buyers to whom independent producers may license their product. As a result, the Producers believe that independent-feature filmmakers and their investors, at least in the near term, are likely if they make a deal with a net-caster to retain greater leverage and creative control over how their films are marketed and released and, in the process, reap higher profits from the intellectual property they create. However, given rapidly changing technological developments and shifting consumer tastes, it is not possible to predict with any certainty, what effect, if any, this or other new distribution channels will have on potential overall revenue for feature-length motion pictures.

Target audience. *XYZ Film* is a feature film geared towards a broad viewing audience and targets major segments of the moviegoing public. The Producers believe that both young and old generations of American moviegoers enjoy films that not only are entertaining but also leave them with a belief of hope in the human spirit.

Dark themes. As evidenced by movies like *Seven* and *The Crow*, darkly themed movies are tailor-made for the eighteen-to-thirty-five-year-old-male demographic.

The Halloween movie. With a PG-13 rating, cost-efficient opportunities to market the Film to the Halloween retail and haunted-attraction industries, the attachment of the Halloween-related Midnight Syndicate brand name and the traditional "Halloween-style" themes of the vampire and zombie, the Producers believe that *XYZ Film* will appeal (and be accessible) to both teenagers (fifteen to eighteen) and their parents (thirty to sixty) during the Halloween season.

Suspense thrillers. The Producers feel that an underlying theme of internal struggle versus interpersonal relationships matched with a female heroine will greatly enhance the Film's potential attractiveness to a female demographic.

The date movie. By combining a dark theme with strong characters and complex relationships, the Producers believe *XYZ Film* has many of the elements to attract the Friday-night date crowd. By appealing to this difficult to target audience, *XYZ Film* may be able to attract a strong cross-over demographic within a wide age range.

The horror-movie community. *XYZ Film* is not a "typical" horror film, especially given the recent trend of many horror films to focus on violence, special effects and gore with less storytelling. The Producers believe that, at the time of this Offering, there is a real demand in the horror-movie community for horror films with good stories that "bend the rules" a bit and offer horror-movie fans something different. The Producers believe that *XYZ Film* Screenplay meets that need.

The Midnight Syndicate fan. Midnight Syndicate's Halloween CDs resemble horror movie scores to imaginary, nonexistent horror films. Most, if not all, consumers of Midnight Syndicate's Halloween CDs are in the target audience of *XYZ Film.* The Producers hope that some will be intrigued by the theme of the movie, others by a curiosity to see a film produced by a musical act they enjoy, still others who, driven by trust in and a loyalty to the brand name, will support any creative endeavor that bears the Midnight Syndicate name including *XYZ Film.*

The art-house crowd. It is also anticipated that the fringe viewers of independent films will be satisfied with the horror theme. The rare and complex relationships among disparate individuals who ultimately depend on each other for survival is the cornerstone of many successful independent films (e.g., *Sideways, Being John Malkovich*).

Box-Office Comparables

The following discussion provides information relating to other films the Producers believe are similar in some respect to the LLC's film. The box-office performances are listed to provide the prospective investor with a relatively current perspective on the films' comparative performances. These revenue totals do not include international sales, home-video/DVD sales, domestic cable or ancillary-market profits. Domestic box-office gross is merely one indicator of a film's overall financial performance. Also, box-office grosses are highly dependent on advertising commitments and release patterns. Some of these films garnered their dollars from a relatively small number of screens while others played much wider. Some received only perfunctory theatrical releases designed to trigger video/DVD, TV and foreign sales. (Overall domestic sales for films has significantly increased with the advent and proliferation of DVD sales and rentals—see "Description of business" under "Market Overview/State of the Industry.") NO ASSURANCES, HOWEVER, CAN BE PROVIDED THAT THE LLC'S FILM WILL PERFORM AS WELL AS ANY OF THE MOTION PICTURES LISTED. Table 7.2 is a list of independent films with some elements that are similar to those of the LLC's Film, along with their domestic box-office grosses.

Table 7.2.
Distributor, estimated budget and domestic box-office
gross for selected independent films, 1995–2005

Year	Title	Distributor	Estimated budget ($ million)	Domestic box-office gross ($)
2005	*Junebug*	Sony Pictures Classics	2.0	2.7
2005	*Me, You & Everyone We Know*	IFC Films	2.0	3.9
2004	*Garden State*	Fox Searchlight	2.5	26.8
2004	*Napoleon Dynamite*	Fox Searchlight	.4	44.5
2003	*All the Real Girls*		2.5	.55
2003	*American Splendor*	HBO Films/Fine Line	2.5	6.1
2003	*Die Mommie Die*	Sundance Film Series	1.0	.312
2003	*Lost in Translation*	Universal/Focus	4.0	31.5
2003	*Northfork*	Paramount Classics	1.9	1.4
2003	*Party Monster*	Strand Releasing	2.0	.718
2003	*Pieces of April*	MGM/UA	.3	2.36
2003	*The Cooler*	Lions Gate	3.8	.675
2003	*The Shape of Things*	Focus Features	4.0	.736
2003	*The Station Agent*	Miramax	.5	5.8
2003	*Thirteen*	Fox Searchlight	1.5	4.6
2002	*Bend It Like Beckham*	20th Century Fox	4.0	32.5
2002	*My Big Fat Greek Wedding*	IFC/Gold Circle	4.5	244
2002	*Raising Victor Vargas*	S. Goldwyn/Fireworks	1.0	2.1
2002	*Spun*	Newmarket	3.5	.412
2001	*The Anniversary Party*	Fine Line	.5	4.1
1998	*Smoke Signals*		2.0	6.9
1995	*Before Sunrise*		2.5	22.5
1995	*Welcome to the Dollhouse*		1.0	4.6

SOURCES: International Distribution Strategies, Baseline, *Variety*, Internet Movie Database, Box Office Mojo and The Numbers.

8. Motion-Picture-Industry Overview

As noted earlier, the courts have determined that active investors need to have specialized knowledge and experience in the industry in which they are being asked to invest (see chapter 1). A strict interpretation of that requirement pretty well eliminates the use of a business plan with prospective investors who have not worked in the film industry; working in the industry is how someone would presumably get knowledge and experience in the applicable industry. Unfortunately, there is likely only a small number of prospective investors who may qualify under these court rules for investing as active investors in a film deal promoted through a business plan. Of course, as noted earlier, people currently working in the film industry do not need to see a business plan. They already know about the industry. They only need to see a producer's package, and again, a producers' package is not the same thing as a business plan.

A third, borderline possibility may include those who are knowledgeable about the film industry even though they have no hands-on experience working in the film industry. If it is possible to raise funds from one to three active investors who are knowledgeable about the film industry, then the question becomes, "How can individuals who are not knowledgeable about the film industry become sufficiently knowledgeable and, therefore, eligible active investors?"

One of the possibilities suggested by the securities regulations themselves is the use of a section in the business plan called the industry overview. In order to help bring those unknowledgeable individuals up to speed, knowledge wise, it may be essential to include in the business plan a "Motion-Picture-Industry Overview." Such a section would provide basic information about how the industry works. It differs from the "Market Overview/State of the Industry" in that the former does not attempt to provide current statistical information. It also differs from the "Description of the Film" in that the industry overview does not discuss the current project for which funding is being sought. It does, however, seek to explain in clear terms what happens during each of the various phases in the life of a motion picture including development, production and distribution. No assurances can be provided here, however, that adding such a section to a business plan will alleviate the court-imposed requirement that those seeking to raise money through the use of a business plan from active investors must limit their solicitation to those who are both knowledgeable and experienced in the film industry

Sample "Motion-Picture-Industry Overview"

Motion-Picture-Industry Overview

This motion-picture-industry overview provides background information regarding the motion-picture industry generally for persons who may not be familiar with such matters. The information set forth in this overview has been prepared by the film producer, but such information may or may not apply to the specific project described in this Business Plan.

General. The theatrical motion-picture industry in the United States has changed substantially over the last three decades and continues to evolve rapidly. Historically, the "major studios" financed, produced and distributed the vast majority of American-made motion pictures seen by most U.S. moviegoers. During the most recent decade, many of the motion pictures released have been produced by so-called independent producers even though some of the production financing for such pictures and distribution funds have been provided by the major studio/distributors. Other independent films are distributed by so-called independent distributors (i.e., those not affiliated with the major studios).

The following general description is a simplified overview of the complex process of producing and distributing motion pictures and is intended to be an aid to investors in understanding the motion-picture business. This overview does not describe what will necessarily occur in the case of any particular motion picture.

Production of motion pictures. During the film-making process, which may take approximately twelve to twenty-four months from the start of the development phase to theatrical release, a film progresses through several stages. The four general stages of motion-picture production are development, preproduction, principal photography and postproduction. A brief summary of each of the four general movie-production stages follows:

- *Development.* In the development stage, underlying literary material for a motion-picture project is acquired, either outright, through an option to acquire such rights or by engaging a writer to create original literary material. If the literary material is not in script form, a writer must be engaged to create a script. The script must be sufficiently detailed to provide the production company and others participating in the financing of a motion picture with enough information to estimate the cost of producing the motion picture. Projects in development often do not become completed motion pictures.

- *Preproduction.* During the preproduction stage, the production company usually selects a director, actors and actresses, prepares a budget and secures the necessary financing. In cases involving unique or desired talent, commitments must be made to keep performers available for the picture. Some preproduction activities may occur during development.
- *Principal photography.* Principal photography is the process of filming a motion picture and is the most costly stage of the production of a motion picture. Principal photography may take twelve weeks or more to complete for some projects. Bad weather at locations, the illness of a cast or crew member, disputes with local authorities or labor unions, a director's or producer's decision to reshoot scenes for artistic reasons and other often unpredictable events can seriously delay the scheduled completion of principal photography and substantially increase its costs. Once a motion picture reaches the principal-photography stage, it usually will be completed.
- *Postproduction.* During the postproduction stage, the editing of the raw footage and the scoring and mixing of dialogue, music and sound effects tracks take place, and master printing elements are prepared.

Distribution of motion pictures. Motion-picture revenue is derived from the worldwide licensing of a motion picture in some or all of the following media: (a) theatrical exhibition, (b) nontheatrical exhibition (viewing in airplanes, hotels, military bases and other facilities), (c) pay television systems for delivery to television receivers by means of cable, over-the-air and satellite delivery systems, (d) commercial television networks, (e) local commercial television stations and (f) reproduction on videocassettes, DVDs (and video discs) for home-video use. The several new technologies including direct-broadcast satellite, video on demand (VOD), near video on demand (NVOD) and the Internet may allow a film to generate additional revenues. Revenue may also be derived from licensing "ancillary rights" to a motion picture for the creation of books, published music, soundtrack albums and merchandise. A picture is not always sold in all of these markets or media.

The timing of revenues received from the various sources differs from film to film (see table 8.1). Typically, theatrical receipts from U.S. distribution are received approximately 90 percent in the first twelve months after a film is first exhibited and 10 percent in the second twelve months. Theatrical receipts from the rest of the world are typically received 40 percent in the first year following initial theatrical release, 50 percent in the second year and 10 percent in the third year. Home-video royalties are typically received 80 percent in the first year following theatrical release and 20 percent in later years. Pay and cable license fees are typically received 65 percent in the third year, 25 percent in the fourth year and 10 percent in the fifth year following theatrical release. The majority of syndicated domestic television receipts are typically received in the fourth, fifth and sixth years after theatrical release if there are no network-television licenses and the sixth, seventh and eighth years if there are network-television licenses. The markets for film products have been undergoing rapid changes due to technological and other innovations. As a consequence, the sources of revenues available have been changing rapidly, and the relative importance of the various markets as well as the timing of such revenues has also changed and can be expected to continue to change.

Table 8.1.
Typical release sequence of feature film through seven years

Distribution channel	Years of movie release						
	1	2	3	4	5	6	7
Domestic theatrical	= =						
Pay per view	= =						
Foreign theatrical	= = = =						
Home video	= = = = = = = = = = = =						
Pay television		+ + +	+ + + + + + + +				
Foreign television		+ +					
Network TV		+ + + + + + + + +					
TV syndication				+ + + + + + + + + +			

SOURCE: LINK Resources, *Off-Hollywood & Entertainment Industry Economics*, 2nd ed.

LEGEND:
= Window with open-ended time periods
+ Window with exclusive runs

Feature-film-release sequence. Movie-release sequences are a function of the marketplace and to some extent the prerogative of individual distributors. Thus, release sequences change as new delivery technology is introduced; these sequences may vary with specific films. As a result of the different time periods during which movies are exhibited and/or viewed in various markets and media, the revenue stream generated by a given movie may typically continue for seven years or more.

In table 8.1, all but home video, network television, the presentation of classic pictures on pay television and television syndication are completed by the end of year two, thus the great percentage of the revenue generated by movies comes during and immediately after the earlier windows, assuming payments are made promptly. Also, the percentages of revenue generated by each market fluctuate from year to year (e.g., foreign has been growing in recent years relative to domestic theatrical). Table 8.1 does not consider the potential revenue from a movie soundtrack album, merchandising possibilities or the film's value as part of a film library.

A summary follows of each of the sources of revenue of motion pictures and the distribution/licensing process associated with such sources:

U.S. theatrical distribution. In recent years, U.S. theatrical exhibition has generated a declining percentage of the total income earned by most pictures, largely because of the increasing importance of cable and pay television, home video and other ancillary markets. Nevertheless, the total revenues generated in the U.S. theatrical market are still substantial and are still likely to account for a large percentage of revenues for a particular film. In addition, performance in the U.S. theatrical market generally also has a profound effect on the value of the picture in other media and markets.

Motion pictures may be distributed to theatrical markets through branch offices. Theatrical distribution requires the commitment of substantial funds in addition to a motion picture's negative cost. The distributor must arrange financing and personnel to: (a) create the motion picture's advertising campaign and distribution plan, (b) disseminate advertising, publicity and promotional material by means of magazines, newspapers, trailers ("coming attractions") and television, (c) duplicate and distribute prints of the motion picture, (d) "book" the motion picture in theaters and (e) collect from exhibitors the distributor's share of the box-office receipts from the motion picture. A distributor must carefully monitor the theaters to which it licenses its picture to ensure that the exhibitor keeps only the amounts to which it is entitled by contract and promptly pays all amounts due to the distributor. Distributors will sometimes reach negotiated settlements with exhibitors as to the amounts to be paid, and such settlements may relate to amounts due for several pictures.

For a picture's initial theatrical release, a U.S. theater exhibitor will usually pay to a distributor a percentage of box-office receipts, which is negotiated based on the expected appeal of the motion picture and the stature of the distributor. The negotiated percentage of box-office receipts remitted to the distributor is generally known as "film rentals" and is typically characterized in distribution agreements as a portion of the distributor's "gross receipts." Such gross receipts customarily diminish during the course of a picture's theatrical run. Typically, the distributor's share of total box-office receipts over the entire initial theatrical release period will average between twenty-five and sixty percent depending on the distributor; the exhibitor will retain the remaining seventy-five to forty percent. [Source: Cones, *Feature Film Distribution Deal*]. The exhibitor will also retain all receipts from the sale of food and drinks at the theater (concessions). Occasionally, an exhibitor will pay to the distributor a flat fee or percentage of box-office receipts against a guaranteed amount. Pay television and new home-entertainment equipment (such as video games, computers, videocassette players and DVD players) offer a more general competitive alternative to motion-picture theatrical exhibition of feature films.

Major film distributors are often granted the right to license exhibition of a film in perpetuity and normally have the responsibility for advertising and supplying prints and other materials to the exhibitors. Under some arrangements, the distributor retains a distribution fee from the gross receipts, which averages approximately 33 percent of the film's gross receipts and recoups the costs incurred in distributing the film [Source: Cones, *Feature Film Distribution Deal*]. The principal costs incurred are the cost of duplicating the digital master into prints for actual exhibition and advertising of the motion picture. The distribution deal usually provides that the parties providing the financing are then entitled to recover the cost of producing the film. However, bank-financed productions will typically require that the bank be paid back its principal, interest and fees out of first monies to the distributor.

Expenses incurred in distributing a motion picture are substantial and vary depending on many factors. These factors include the initial response by the public to the motion picture, the nature of its advertising campaign, the pattern of its release (e.g., the number of theaters booked and the length of time that a motion picture is in release). The amount film distributors spend on prints and advertising is generally left to the discretion of the distributor. In some instances, however, the producer may negotiate minimum expenditures or ceilings on such items.

Foreign theatrical distribution. Although the value of the foreign theatrical market changes due to currency exchange rate fluctuations and the political conditions in the world or specific territories, it continues to provide a significant source of revenue for theatrical distribution. In recent years, foreign theatrical revenues have often been accountable for more than 50 percent of a domestically produced U.S. film's gross theatrical revenue. Due to the fact that this market comprises a multiplicity of countries and, in some cases, requires the making of foreign-language versions, the distribution pattern stretches over a longer period of time than does exploitation of a film in the U.S. theatrical market. Major studio/distributors usually distribute motion pictures in foreign countries through local entities. These local entities generally will be either wholly owned by the distributor, a joint venture between the distributor and another motion-picture company or an independent agent or subdistributor. Such local entities may also distribute motion pictures of other producers, including other major studios. Film-rental agreements with foreign exhibitors take a number of different forms, but they typically provide for payment to a distributor of a fixed percentage of box-office receipts or a flat amount. Risks associated with foreign distribution include fluctuations in currency values and government restrictions or quotas on the percentage of receipts that may be paid to the distributor, the remittance of funds to the United States and the importation of motion pictures into a foreign country.

New technologies in distribution and delivery. High-tech movie megaplexes are changing the very landscape of the domestic- and foreign-distribution market-places, especially in France, Italy, Eastern Europe and Russia. In the U.S. market, which started the trend, giant cineplexes or megaplexes with ten to twelve screens per complex, have forever replaced the local single- or three-screen theaters. Movies encoded as digital files, either recorded on optical disc and physically shipped or broadcast via satellite or land line, are expected to replace film prints as the preferred method for distributing movies to theaters. This assumes also that audience-acceptable digital-projection technology will develop and be installed.

Home-video rights. Since its inception, the home-video market in the United States has experienced substantial growth in the last decade. Certain foreign territories, particularly Europe, have seen an increased use of home-video units due to the relative lack of diversified television programming, although those circumstances have been changing also. Consequently, sales of videocassettes have increased in such markets in recent years. Although growth in this area may be reduced because of an increase in television programming in such foreign territories, receipts from home video or DVD in these markets can be expected to continue to be significant.

Films are generally released on home video six to nine months after initial domestic theatrical release of the picture but before the exhibition of the picture on cable/pay or network television.

Domestic-television distribution. Television rights in the United States are generally licensed first to pay television for an exhibition period following home-video release, thereafter to network television for an exhibition period, then to pay television again and finally syndicated to independent stations. Therefore, the owner of a film may receive payments resulting from television licenses over a period of six years or more.

Domestic cable and pay television. Pay-television rights include rights granted to cable, direct-broadcast satellite, microwave, pay per view and other services paid for by subscribers. Cable and pay-television networks usually license pictures for initial exhibition commencing six to twelve months after initial domestic the-atrical release, as well as for subsequent showings. Pay television services such as Home Box Office Inc. (HBO) and Showtime/The Movie Channel Inc. (Showtime) have entered into output contracts with one or more major production companies on an exclusive or nonexclusive basis to assure themselves a continuous supply of motion-picture programming. Some pay-television services have required exclusivity as a precondition to such contracts.

The pay-television market is characterized by a large number of sellers and few buyers. However, the number of motion pictures utilized by these buyers is significantly large, and a great majority of motion pictures that receive theatrical exhibition in the United States are, in fact, shown on pay television.

Domestic network television. In the United States, broadcast-network rights are granted to ABC, CBS, NBC or other entities formed to distribute programming to a large group of stations. The commercial-television networks in the United States license motion pictures for a limited number of exhibitions during a period that usually commences two to three years after a motion picture's initial theatrical release. During recent years, only a small percentage of motion pictures have been licensed to network television, and the fees paid for such motion pictures have declined. This decline is generally attributed to the growth of the pay television and home-video markets, and the ability of commercial television networks to produce and acquire made-for-television motion pictures at a lower cost than license fees previously paid for theatrical motion pictures.

Domestic television syndication. Distributors also license the right to broadcast a motion picture on local, commercial television stations in the United States, usually for a period commencing five years after initial theatrical release of the motion picture but earlier if the producer has not entered into a commercial-television-network license. This activity, known as "syndication," has become an important source of revenues as the competition for programming among local television stations has increased.

Foreign-television syndication. Motion pictures are now being licensed in the foreign-television market in a manner similar to that in the United States. The number of foreign television stations as well as the modes of transmission (i.e., pay, cable, network, satellite, and others) have been increasing quickly, and the value of such markets has been likewise increasing and should continue to expand.

Producers may license motion pictures to foreign television stations during the same period they license such motion pictures to television stations in the United States; however, governmental restrictions and the timing of the initial foreign theatrical release of the motion pictures in the territory may delay the exhibition of such motion pictures in such territory.

Nontheatrical distribution. In addition to the markets and media discussed above, the owner of a film may also be able to license the rights for nontheatrical uses to specialized distributors who, in turn, make the film available to airlines, hotels, schools, offshore oil rigs, public libraries, prisons, community groups, the armed forces and ships at sea.

The Internet and broadband access. Recent technological advances such as digital satellite transmission, cable modems and DSL, all geared to high-speed broadband Internet access, provide another potential revenue source for feature films. In the near future there may be several "Net-casters" with the ability to release and distribute a theatrical quality, full-length motion picture over the Internet, on a global basis, essentially bypassing traditional distributors, with their high costs and fee structures.

Relicensing. The collective retained rights in a group of previously produced motion pictures is often a key asset, as such pictures may be relicensed in pay and commercial television, home-video and nontheatrical markets and occasionally re-released for theatrical exhibition.

Although no one can be certain of the value of these rights, certain older films retain considerable popularity and may be relicensed for theatrical or television exhibition. New technologies brought about by the continuing improvements in electronics may also give rise to new forms of exhibition that will develop value in the future.

Other ancillary markets. A distributor may earn revenues from other ancillary sources unless the necessary exploitation rights in the underlying literary property have been retained by writers, talent, composers or other third parties. The right to use the images of characters in a motion picture may be licensed for merchandising items such as toys, T-shirts and posters. Motion-picture rights may also be licensed for novelizations of the screenplay, comic-book versions of the screenplay and books about the making of the motion picture. The soundtrack of a motion picture may be separately licensed for soundtrack records and may generate revenue in the form of mechanical performance royalties, public-performance royalties and sheet-music publication royalties.

9. Financial Information

Financial information is another section of a traditional business plan that is confusing, partly because of the varying titles used or recommended. The more general title "Financial Information" is often used and can work because it covers all possibilities within the topic. Some business-plan consultants suggest that this section be referred to as "Financial Documents," a section that would summarize all of the financial records showing past, current and projected finances. On the other hand, not all of the financial information that may be included exists in the form of a document that can be summarized. The title "Financial Plan" implies that the section will discuss the overall plan for financing the costs associated with developing, producing or distributing the motion picture, recognizing that some of the "plan" may include financing from other sources, that may be combined with the investor financing being sought through the business plan (i.e., the equity component). Thus, "Financial Plan" may work best as a subsection, as opposed to the main-section heading.

Of course, a "Financial History" section title suggests that information relating to the past financing arrangements of the company, if there is such a history, will be disclosed here. Thus, "Financial History" may also work best as a subsection of the "Financial Information" section. As noted above, the projected financial results of an investment could also be included in a broad "Financial Information" section, although it may work better to set out these financial projections separately as an exhibit to the business plan, since, as mentioned earlier, the financial projections are often prepared by a third party, and the pagination becomes more complicated. In any case, past financial information relating to the company or business venture, its current financial status, the overall financial plan and the projected financial results should either be included here or referenced in this section. For example, there may be a paragraph that talks about the financial projections and refers to the inclusion of those projections as an exhibit to the business plan.

Financial history. This possible subsection of "Financial Information" should first include a brief discussion of how the company or business venture has been funded to this point. If the business is a complete start-up, there will be little to talk about. If the production/development company has existed for some time, an explanation as to how it has financed its operations to date would be appropriate. For example, if the company is a sole proprietorship or a general partnership, the filmmaker may want to point out that the owner or owners have contributed a specified amount of cash, property or services to fund the company's activities thus far. If it is an existing member-managed LLC, the discussion will relate to who the members are and what consideration they have contributed for their interests. If the company and investment vehicle is to be a corporation to be formed upon funding, again, there is no existing company whose financing to date can be disclosed. If on the other hand, an individual producer has already expended a sum of money to acquire rights to a film project and intends to transfer those rights to the corporation or other entity once created and be reimbursed for that expense, a statement to that effect may be inserted here.

Supplemental funding. In the current independent-film marketplace, it is not uncommon for several different sources of financing to be needed in order to fully fund a film project. So, if in addition to the funding being sought through the use of the business plan, the producers have already made or intend to make arrangements for partial financing from other sources (e.g., foreign presales, domestic negative pickup, coproduction, cash flowing tax incentives, and the like), those arrangements should also be disclosed here in this section. If such funding is not in place (i.e., not in a bank account controlled by the producers) or is contingent upon the business-plan solicitation for investor funds being successful, those contingencies should also be disclosed to the filmmaker's current prospective investors.

Financial plan. As noted above, the overall plan to finance the film may be discussed under this subsection, which is closely related to the above subsection heading "Supplemental Funding." For example, a producer might set out a financial plan as follows:

Line items	Percentage (%)
Equity component (investor raise)	45
Bank loans based on foreign presale commitments	20
Cash advances on state tax incentives	15
Gap financing	10
Cast or crew deferrals	10

The line items in a film's financial plan and the percentages may change to reflect the needs and opportunities for each project. Among the many other possible partial-funding sources that could appear in a film's financial plan are government subsidies, international coproductions, personal loans, gifts, grants, and similar sources. Again, if the production of the film is contingent on all financial elements being in place, that needs to be disclosed to the prospective investors.

Use of proceeds. This very important major subsection of the "Financial Information" section includes an explanation to prospective investors regarding how the filmmaker anticipates using their invested funds. This subsection does not require as much detail as might appear in a film budget but should be something more akin to the top sheet of the budget, plus any expenses incurred in putting together and marketing the business plan (i.e., the costs associated with raising the money). Note that these costs of raising the money (copying and binding of the business plan, art work for the cover, marketing costs, finder's fees, fees for consultants, and other expenses) are not part of the film's budget and should be set out separately so the investors can know that the producer is not spending an unreasonable amount of money on fund-raising (i.e., the cost of money).

Film budget costs to be used in a business plan should be based on the best available information and be as accurate as possible. Many individuals in the film industry have bona fide expertise in preparing film budgets. In addition, several software programs for film budgeting are available as well as books on the subject. Most film schools also teach film budgeting. Of course, using an experienced line producer to break down a script to get a good solid film budget may cost money but could be the best option. That's one of the reasons why independent filmmakers sometimes raise money for the development phase of a film to pay for that kind of professional help. Few film-producer misdeeds are potentially more damaging to the relationship between investors and film producers than for the estimated film budget to be significantly off the mark. Starting the production process and getting other people to make arrangements and time commitments only to run out of funds are also damaging to a filmmaker's reputation in the film community.

Although not mandated for a business plan, the securities terminology for this subsection is "Use of Proceeds." To make it clear to prospective investors that these are just estimates of how the investor funds will be used and made at the time of the preparation of the business plan, it may be helpful to add the word "Estimated" to the subsection title so it reads, "Estimated Use of Proceeds." It is also helpful in that regard to add language following the estimated use of proceeds reminding the prospective investors that these estimates are tentative (see sample language below in "Estimated Use of Proceeds").

Line items such as distributor delivery items, marketing to distributors, investment-vehicle operating expenses and profit-participation auditor are also potential film-related expenses that may be included in the estimated use of proceeds section of the business plan, but not included in the film's budget (see sample "Estimated Use of Proceeds" below). Be careful when converting the film's budget top-sheet information to an estimated use of proceeds to be sure that these nonbudget items are set out separately from the budget items and not overlooked. In other words, the concept of estimated use of proceeds for a business plan is broader than a summary or top sheet of the film's budget because there are some cost items that need to be included in the estimated use of proceeds subsection that are not properly part of the film budget. So, it is important for filmmakers to understand that when a filmmaker is working on drafting this subsection of a business plan, he or she is no longer just preparing a summary of the anticipated film-budget costs (i.e., other expenses or uses of investor funds will need to be included).

Management and affiliate compensation. This important subsection of information required to be disclosed in a securities disclosure document and, by analogy, useful for informing prospective investors through a business plan includes disclosures regarding the various ways in which the management and individual affiliates will be compensated, particularly out of the film's budget. The term "affiliate" is commonly one of those defined terms, the definition for which is often found in an entity's formation documents (e.g., an LLC operating agreement or the partnership agreement of a limited partnership). The term typically refers to any person or entity directly or indirectly controlling, controlled by or under common control with the investment vehicle or its managing entity. Determining who management and the affiliates are depends on the choice of investment vehicle. So, if the investment vehicle is:

- *an investor financing agreement,* the individual or entity serving as one of the parties to that contract with the investor would be considered management, and all forms of his or her proposed compensation, if any, ought to be disclosed in the business plan. If that party to the investor financing agreement other than the investor is some form of company, then the compensation to be paid to the owners of that company ought to be disclosed.
- *a joint venture agreement,* the compensation to be paid to the joint-venture partner other than the individual or entity making the cash investment ought to be disclosed in this subsection of the business plan.
- *a corporation (to be formed upon funding),* the corporation itself would be considered management and its various forms of compensation ought to be disclosed in the business plan. In addition, any compensation to be paid to any of the corporation's proposed owners, particularly the majority owners or those controlling more than 10 percent of the corporation's shares should be disclosed.

- *a member-managed LLC*, the compensation proposed to be paid to the LLC itself and its owners (some of whom are likely to be cash investors) should be disclosed.

When raising money for a film to be produced, there are multiple opportunities to compensate such individuals and entities, such as an organization fee for services provided in organizing the entity or a management fee for services provided in managing the entity. In both cases, since there are so many other opportunities for filmmakers to be compensated for working on a film project, these two fees are often waived by the people involved. Investors tend to view such waivers favorably.

It may also be permissible for management or the individuals involved to be reimbursed for their out-of-pocket expenses incurred in organizing the entity or investment vehicle and putting together and marketing the business plan to prospective investors. It's probably a good idea to place a ceiling or limit on the amount of such reimbursement so that the filmmaker's prospective investors know that he or she is being reasonable about such expenditures.

The management and affiliates may also have some sort of profit participation in the revenue stream of the film. Again, the exact terminology used depends on the investment vehicle. For example, a production company using the investor financing agreement, may offer a 90/10 split (in favor of the investor) of the production company's gross revenues received from the exploitation of the film until the investor recoups at some defined level (e.g., the investor receives 120 percent of his, her, its or their original capital investment). So during that period of time while the investor is attempting to recoup his/her/its/their investment, the production company will be paid 10 percent of that revenue stream. Such profit participations to management, whether the production company or a specific individual, need to be disclosed in the business plan so prospective investors will be fully informed about the proposed deal. The same arrangement may apply to a joint venture.

Note here that there is no mention about the payment of any interest. That is because interest payments are associated with loans, not investments. A filmmaker offers investors an opportunity to recoup their investments and, everyone hopes, a return on their investment in addition to recoupment—but not interest.

Traditionally, profit participations for management of a corporation are handled as dividends paid to shareholders. Thus, if management also owns shares, it will be paid dividends right along with the other shareholders. Corporate dividends are paid out of a corporation's earnings strictly in accordance with the ownership percentages of the shareholders but at the discretion of the corporation's board of directors. It is more difficult to explain to investors that the corporation's management will be paid some percentage of the corporation's revenues prior to the declaration of dividends, although it can be done. On the other hand, such an arrangement is very likely to make it more difficult to sell the deal to investors. Thus, it may turn out to be the proverbial "shooting yourself in the foot."

A member-managed LLC offers greater flexibility in structuring these profit participations for selected individuals, although all of the member-managed LLC's members are by definition considered to be management. They are, after all, member-managers. Any profit participation to be paid to such individuals for their services relating to, for example, producing the film, directing the film or writing the screenplay, not only need to be disclosed in the business plan but also would have to be authorized by the LLC's operating agreement, which, in turn, needs to be approved by all of the member-managers.

It may also be important to disclose what interest anyone or any entity considered to be management or an affiliate has in any available tax deductions or credits. This may be particularly important if the plan is partly based on international, federal or state tax incentives.

Finally, it is clearly important to disclose what compensation will be paid to any management or affiliated individuals out of the film's budget. In other words, if someone who is an owner or affiliate of the production company is also serving as the producer, director, screenwriter, actor or in another other capacity with respect to the production of the movie, any planned salary to be paid to such individual needs to be disclosed in this paragraph, so again, the prospective investors will know in advance of their decision to invest. In independent film deals, it is common for some of those salaries to be deferred (i.e., not paid during production of the film but paid out of some defined stage in the film's revenue stream, for example, after investor recoupment). These deferred salaries need to be disclosed, too. To protect the investors, deferments may be capped (i.e., limited to an overall specified dollar amount for all cast and crew deferments).

It is important to disclose all forms of compensation to be paid to the people involved in putting the business venture together because they are in a conflict of interest position. Thus, the investors have a right to know what money will be taken out of the deal at what time by whom. Management and affiliates could choose to pay themselves significant amounts of money out of a film's budget for various activities or from that category dealing with the costs of putting together the business plan, combined with various profit-participation opportunities. However, to the extent that the prospective investors get the impression that these individuals or entities are being greedy (i.e., "front-loading"), that will typically stop the deal dead in its tracks. So, it is important for the filmmakers to carefully consider such compensation and try to be more than fair with the investors—after all, the project won't go forward without the investors. In effect, what is being suggested is that filmmakers preparing business plans should not only disclose all forms of compensation to be paid because the investors have a right to know this but do whatever he or she can to make the financial plan attractive to investors (i.e., investor-oriented). Don't front-end load the deal.

Insurance. An independent producer may want to provide some further reassurance to investors by informing them in the business plan about his or her plans to properly insure against certain risks.[1] Traditionally, such reassurance comes in the form of various insurance coverages, often referred to in the film industry as the producer's production insurance package. In the process of preparing the film budget, the independent producer will need to select an insurance broker or agent, determine what coverages are advisable and available, along with the cost, so that when the funds become available, the producer will be able to obtain the needed insurance coverage. The filmmaker will also want to talk to the insurance agent or broker about what arrangements need to be made to add the active investors to the policies as additional insureds.

Completion bond. The producers on a film production will need to determine whether it makes sense to purchase a completion bond for the project. A completion bond is a surety purchased through completion guarantors, specialized companies that for a fee, furnish a written contract that guarantees a motion picture will be finished and delivered on schedule and within budget. Some films produced and financed by the major studio/distributors are, in effect, self-guaranteed, and thus do not require bonding (although others do). The films financed through entertainment lenders always require completion bonds. The producer usually secures a completion guaranty for the benefit of the bank or other financiers who agree to make the necessary production funding available to the producer. Most independently produced films do not obtain a completion guaranty, if for no other reason because of the cost. Completion guarantor fees usually equal at least 3 percent of a film's budget and more under some circumstances. A completion bond, however, does provide the producer with another device to protect an investor from the specific risk of not completing the motion picture. Of course, should a bond be invoked, the completion guarantor may assume control over the production and be in a recoupment position superior to all investors. There is also the risk that if the bond is called upon, and the completion guarantor takes over the production process, the film may not end up being the same picture originally envisioned by the creative team. So, the decision for an independent filmmaker is not clear-cut. The advantages of obtaining a completion bond have to be weighed against the disadvantages for each project being considered.

Investment matters. Another part of the "Financial Information" section may be referred to as "Investment Matters" or some other similar but suitable heading. Securities disclosure documents typically use the title "Terms of the Offering" for this information. The concept for this subsection is to explain to prospective investors just how the deal is structured, that is, what the investment vehicle is and how the investors are supposed to get their money back and, all hope, make a profit (reserving the details of the revenue flow for the financial projections). Some business-plan consultants refer to this latter issue as an "exit strategy" (a plan that allows the investors to recoup their invested capital, make a profit and terminate their equity position in the enterprise). As with so many other parts of a business plan, exit strategies vary with different investment vehicles and may offer optional opportunities for investors to exit.

An investor financing agreement is a contract between the producer of the film and the investor(s). It typically sets out the contributions of each of the parties. For example, the producer may contribute the script or the rights optioned or acquired. It also offers the investor(s) a profit participation in a defined stage of the film's revenue stream (e.g., 50 percent of the net revenues actually received by the production company). Since it is one of the active-investor options, it should set out the manner in which the investor(s) will be actively involved in helping make the important decisions associated with the project.[2] As the project moves forward, it may be a good idea to document the active investor's participation, to guard against any future claim that the investor was not really active, and thus an unregistered security had been sold.

A joint-venture agreement is also a contract between the producer of the film and the investor. It is more commonly used when the production company and the active investor are both entities, as opposed to individuals. Most of the domestic coproductions are typically structured as joint ventures. The joint-venture agreement typically sets out the contributions of each of the parties. For example, the production company may contribute the script or the rights optioned or acquired. It also offers the investor(s) a profit participation in a defined stage of the film's revenue stream. Again, since it is one of the active-investor options, it should set out the manner in which the investor will be actively involved in helping make the important decisions associated with the project.[3] Of course, if the joint-venture partner making the financial contribution is not knowledgeable and experienced in the film industry as required by law, even an interest in a joint venture may be considered a security.[4]

The initial incorporation strategy involves bringing together a small group of people, some contributing cash and others contributing property such as a script. Each individual will be a founding shareholder of the corporation to be formed. As shareholders, they have the right to determine who will serve on the corporation's board of directors. That decision is made at the shareholder's first annual meeting and is reflected in the minutes of that meeting. These shareholders will continue to be involved at each annual shareholders' meeting in determining who serves on the corporation's board of directors. The board of directors, in turn, determines the corporation's policies and hires its officers. Some of those founding shareholders may serve on the board. The officers direct the day-to-day activities of the corporation. Some of the corporation's officers may be drawn from that same group of founding shareholders.

These paragraphs in the business plan relating to use of the corporate investment vehicle may also include some discussion of whether the corporation will seek to qualify as an S corporation and, therefore, not have to pay corporate federal income taxes at the entity level, or whether it will remain a regular C corporation.

Note that the process of incorporating involves the preparation and filing of articles of incorporation with the secretary of state in the state chosen for incorporation. That is not the end of the formation process, however. Once the articles are filed and approved, the corporation must hold the first of its shareholder annual meetings and the initial meeting of the board of directors. Minutes must be prepared in support of both of those meetings. The minutes for the shareholders meeting should reflect who has been chosen to serve on the corporation's board of directors. The minutes for the board of directors meeting should reflect that the corporation's bylaws, its corporate seal and the form of stock certificate have been approved, who has been elected as officers, the corporation's accounting period, arrangements for a bank account, payment of organizational expenses and authorization and issuance of shares (showing who the shareholders are, what consideration was paid and the number of shares purchased). In addition, in order to complete the corporate organization process, the share certificates have to actually be issued to the respective shareholders so those can be kept with each individual shareholder's important papers (not remain with the corporation). The issuance of shares is also recorded on the corporation's stock-transfer ledger, and the minutes are filed with the rest of the corporation's documents, possibly in a "corporate kit."

If a member-managed LLC is to serve as the investment vehicle associated with the business plan, a brief explanation of how the member-managed LLC is to be formed and how it will operate pursuant to the LLC's operating agreement may be included in this subsection of the business plan.

As previously noted, some business-plan consultants recommend that this section be omitted and that such matters be left to negotiation between the prospective investor and the filmmakers. The pros and cons of that advice have already been discussed (see "Deferring decisions and negotiating later" in chapter 1). So, assuming the decision is to include this information, it should clearly explain the nature of the investment vehicle, whether it is an investor financing agreement, a joint-venture agreement, a corporation to be formed or a member-managed LLC. Remember, if the filmmaker chooses another investment vehicle, one involving passive investors (selling shares in an existing corporation or units in a limited partnership or manager-managed LLC), he or she should not be preparing a business plan but instead a securities disclosure document (see "Business plan or securities disclosure document" in chapter 1).

In those situations where the investor or investors are being asked to invest in a film project as opposed to the production company (i.e., participate in the revenue stream generated by the exploitation of the film in all markets and media), the business-plan preparer should make it clear by including a prominent (bold and all caps) disclaimer that the investor is not investing in the company (see such disclaimer under "Investor Percentage Participation" in the sample section at the end of this chapter).

In addition, some independent producers find it helpful to include some sort of investor-incentive scheme to encourage larger investments. Such a scheme is set out under "Investor Incentive Levels" of the sample section at the end of this chapter).

Also, an example of a few paragraphs that refer to the financial projections appearing as an exhibit is included.

Sample of Selected Elements of "Financial Information"

Once again, please note that the sample language offered throughout this book has been borrowed from a variety of sources, thus the names of the production company, the amount of money being sought, the unit size and other variables may differ from example to example. Each filmmaker using such sample language as a basis for drafting a new business plan will have to carefully edit and modify such variables to fit his or her particular situation.

Estimated Use of Proceeds

The Proceeds of this Offering will be used to pay the expenses associated with the organization of the LLC and the conduct of the Offering and to finance the production of the Picture as well as possibly a portion of the films' marketing and promotion. Table 9.1 sets forth the current estimated use of the Offering Proceeds upon the sale of the Minimum of 3 Units at $2,000,000 per Unit ($6,000,000) or the Maximum of 3.5 Units at $2,000,000 per Unit ($7,000,000). A portion of the savings reflected in the Minimum column may be achieved through the use of Deferments (i.e., the delay of payment of some or a portion of the budgeted salaries or other compensation to providers of goods or services in the production of the Film). Such Deferments are not paid out of the Film's budget (i.e., the Offering Proceeds) but instead are paid out of the Film's revenue stream, if any (i.e., the LLC's Distributable Cash), typically after Investor Recoupment (although the LLC has reserved the right to pay deferments to selected Creative Talent prior to Recoupment). Parties agreeing to such Deferments assume the risk that they will not be paid. The amount of such Deferments do not vary with the amount of Offering Proceeds.

The Estimated Use of Proceeds of the Offering is intended to reflect the Producers' best estimates of all costs of organizing the LLC, selling the limited-

Table 9.1.
Estimated use of proceeds

	Minimum[1] ($)	Maximum[2] ($)
Story and other rights	55,500	65,500
Producer's unit	154,028	174,028
Director's unit	151,788	161,788
Cast/casting	907,754	1,392,254
Above-the-line fringes	35,000	44,000
Total above-the-line	1,304,070	1,837,570
Production salaries	523,352	672,275
Extra talent	84,140	95,392
Set design	157,750	165,000
Set construction	110,501	120,788
Set striking	20,000	32,000
Set operations	161,248	178,456
Special effects	30,000	42,000
Set dressing	141,574	154,740
Property	80,846	84,432
Wardrobe	178,704	189,000
Action props: picture vehicles and animals	20,000	30,000
Makeup and hairdressing	90,423	92,500
Lighting and grips	177,835	184,000
Camera	205,433	213,000
Production sound	85,340	92,000
Transportation	519,523	532,000
Locations/permits	430,441	452,000
Travel and living expenses	152,280	163,390
Production film and lab	150,089	160,432
Second unit	50,000	57,500
Tests and reshoots	5,000	9,790
Production period fringes	51,000	66,000
Total production period	3,425,479	3,786,695
Special photographic EFX	100,000	110,000
Editing and projection	252,615	265,000
Music 75,000	85,000	
Sound (postproduction)	107,550	120,000
Postproduction film and lab	155,786	160,000
Titles and opticals	12,000	14,000
Total postproduction	702,951	754,000
Publicity	30,000	40,000
Insurance and medical	110,000	122,800
Legal	35,000	38,935
Contingency	200,000	210,000
Total other	375,000	411,735
Total above-the-line	1,304,070	1,837,570
Total below-the-line	4,128,530	4,540,695

Total above- and below-the-line	5,432,500	6,378,265
Total other	375,000	411,735
FILM BUDGET TOTAL	5,807,500	6,790,000
Marketing to distributors	150,000	160,000
LLC operating expense	12,500	20,000
Offering expenses[3]		
Organizational[4]	10,000	10,000
Syndication[5]	20,000	20,000
Total offering expenses (ceiling)	30,000	30,000
Gross offering proceeds	6,000,000[6]	7,000,000

NOTES: 1. The Minimum plus creative Deferments, if any, will allow the LLC to acquire rights to the Script, produce the Film and market it to film festivals and prospective distributors.

2. The Maximum plus Deferments, if any, will allow the LLC to acquire the rights to the Script, to use more-advanced technology, attract better-known actors, improve resources (such as locations, set dressings, music, and the like) and market the film more aggressively. If an amount between the Minimum and Maximum is raised, the Member-Managers will exercise their discretion in determining how much to expend on the production of the Picture in each of the above-listed production-cost categories and determine in what categories Deferments will be required. Such Deferments, if any, will be paid after Investor Recoupment.

3. Offering expenses for the Offering will paid out of the Offering Proceeds but will not exceed $30,000, thus a high percentage of the monies raised by virtue of the Offering will contribute directly to the quality of the motion picture that ultimately appears on the screen and its marketing. A portion of the Offering expenses will be used to create the LLC.

4. Please see the definition of Organizational Expenses in the Glossary of the Operating Agreement at Exhibit A (see "Member-Manager Compensation" at "Offering Information").

5. Please see the definition of Syndication Expenses in the Glossary section of the Operating Agreement at Exhibit A. The original Member-Managers plan to sell Units directly to investors, and no transaction-related remuneration will be paid to such persons for the sale of Units (see "Plan for Distribution of Units").

6. After the Closing of the segregated interest-bearing bank account created to hold Subscriber funds and until such funds are needed as described in this section, cash on hand may be temporarily invested in short-term, interest-bearing financial instruments guaranteed or insured by the United States Government or its agencies. Interest earned on the Investor funds held until Closing will be paid to the Investors.

liability company interests and producing the Picture up to and including the delivery of the required elements to the Distributor for the LLC's Film. These estimates are made at the time of the preparation of this Business Plan and are necessarily tentative ones. Other than as stated herein, the Producers make no representations with respect to the final cost of any items (including those specified above) relating to the production of the Picture. The Producers reserve the right to modify the budget of the LLC's Picture to adapt to changing contingencies, so long as in the judgment of the Producers, such budget changes improve the LLC's ability to produce a better Picture.

Compensation of Member-Managers

The following list summarizes the form and estimated amounts of compensation, fees and percentage participations to be paid to the LLC Member-Managers and their Affiliates. Such items have not been determined by arm's-length negotiations (see "Operating Agreement"). Other than as set forth herein, in the Operating Agreement and in the Estimated Use of Proceeds section of the Business Plan, no other compensation or remuneration in any form is to be paid to the Member-Managers or their Affiliates.

> *Organization fee.* The Member-Managers have waived any right to receive an LLC Organization Fee for services rendered in connection with the organization of the LLC.
>
> *Reimbursement of expenses.* The Member-Managers have, and will during the course of this Offering, advanced necessary funds for LLC organizational and offering expenses, and those individuals will be reimbursed for such expenses out of the Gross Offering Proceeds. Such reimbursement shall not exceed a ceiling of $30,000.
>
> *Management fee.* The Member-Managers have waived any right to receive an LLC management fee for services rendered in connection with ongoing management of the LLC.
>
> *Interest in distributable cash.* One Hundred percent (100%) of the LLC's Distributable Cash will be paid to the Member-Managers who will share such distributions on a pro rata basis.
>
> *Interest in tax items.* The Member-Managers will also share LLC Losses and tax deductions for income-tax purposes on a pro rata basis.
>
> *Film budget items.* The individual Member-Manager Tim Burnson will be paid $ _____ out of the Film's budget for his scriptwriting services. The individual Member-Manager Peter Knarley will be paid $ _____ out of the Film's budget for his service as Producer, and J. T. Nixon will be paid $ _____ out of the Film's budget for his services as Director.

No other compensation in any form shall be paid to the Member-Managers, or any of their Affiliates, except as set out above. At the conclusion of the LLC, however, all property rights and ancillary rights in the Picture shall revert to and be distributed to the Producer.

Production insurance. The LLC intends to obtain various available insurance coverages to protect the production company and its investors against specified risks that commonly confront filmmakers. In addition, the Producers represent that the LLC's active investor member-managers will each be added to such insurance policies as additional insureds.

Investment Matters

INVESTMENT VEHICLE

This business plan is specifically drafted to offer flexibility to both the producer group and the prospective active investors in choosing the specific investment vehicle. Those options may include (1) an investor financing agreement—a contract between the producer group and the investors that offers a percentage participation in a defined stage of the revenue's generated by the exploitation of the Movies in all markets and media (including any distributor advance, if any); (2) a joint venture between the producer group and an investor group organized as a single entity; (3) incorporation of a small group of investors with the individual producers, with all of such investors serving as founding shareholders of the new entity or (4) an active-investor limited-liability company (member-managed LLC). In order to protect the active status of such investors, the investment vehicle chosen will have to provide for the regular involvement of such investors in the making of important decisions relating to the business activity proposed herein.

[Note that the above example took the approach that the investor and producer could determine the investment vehicle. Further, the following example of an investor-incentive program did not come from the same example as the above "Investment Vehicle" discussion.]

INVESTOR INCENTIVE LEVELS—PATRONS' CIRCLE:
1 TO 3 UNITS PURCHASED ($50,000—$150,000)

- Invitation for limited behind-the-scenes access to observe the production of *XYZ Film* on no more than two days. The specific days will be chosen at the discretion of the Manager. The Manager reserves the right to limit access as per the dictates of set protocol and safety.
- Two VIP tickets to the premiere of *XYZ Film*.
- A signed poster by cast and above-the-line crew.
- A DVD copy of the Film.

ASSOCIATE PRODUCER LEVEL:
4 TO 9 UNITS PURCHASED ($200,000—$450,000)

- Associate Producer credit in the Film's credits.
- A signed poster by cast and above-the-line crew.
- Photograph with the lead actors of *XYZ Film*.
- A DVD copy of the Film.
- Invitation for full VIP behind-the-scenes access to the set for no more than four days during the production of the Film. This includes a limited opportunity to sit in the video village and observe the production close-up. The specific days will be chosen at the discretion of the Manager.

The Manager reserves the right to limit access as per the dictates of set protocol and safety.

- Two seats to a single test screening of *XYZ Film*.
- Four VIP tickets to the premiere of *XYZ Film*.

EXECUTIVE PRODUCER LEVEL:
10+ UNITS PURCHASED ($500,000 AND ABOVE)

- Executive Producer credit in the Film's credits.
- A signed poster by cast and above-the-line crew.
- Photograph with the lead actors of *XYZ Film*.
- Two "extra" appearances in the final scene of the Film, subject to Director's approval.
- Invitation for unlimited VIP behind-the-scenes access throughout the entire production of *XYZ Film*. This includes the opportunity to sit in the video village and observe the production close-up. The Manager reserves the right to limit access as per the dictates of set protocol and safety.
- Private VIP tour of the postproduction process, including an invitation to all test screenings.
- Six VIP tickets to the premiere of *XYZ Film*.
- Lifetime tickets to all future premieres of XYZ Productions LLC.

INVESTOR PERCENTAGE PARTICIPATION

As consideration for providing funding for the Picture, the Investor(s) (or joint-venture partner) will have an equity ownership interest in the Movie described herein that will entitle such Investor(s) to recoup 125 percent of his, her, their or its investment out of the net revenues received by the Production Company for the acquisition and/or exploitation of the Picture in all markets and media, and after this defined level of Investor Recoupment has been achieved, a 50 percent percentage participation in all net revenues actually received by the Production Company in relation to the exploitation of the Picture.

AN INVESTMENT BY AN INVESTOR IN THE PROJECT DESCRIBED HEREIN DOES NOT CONSTITUTE A DIRECT INVESTMENT IN THE PRODUCTION COMPANY.

[Note that this example of investor percentage participation is inconsistent with the corporate investment-vehicle option.]

FINANCING STRATEGY AND SAMPLE REVENUE PROJECTIONS

The Producers for the Picture have chosen to finance the production through a member-managed limited-liability company Offering to active investors. This structure offers flexibility in regard to Deferring pay to creative personnel and giving profit-sharing incentives to investors. Before utilizing investor monies the original Member-Managers are required to raise the Minimum Offering

Proceeds ($500,000). If the Minimum is raised, the Script will be acquired by the LLC, and *XYZ Film* will be produced.

The Sample Revenue Projections appearing at Exhibit D are not necessarily based on conditions and courses of action that the Producers believe are necessarily the expected results of operations for the period projected. They illustrate what would happen if certain assumptions upon which the projections are based do occur. Some but not all of these assumptions are based on projected figures for the year 2010 and beyond which have been prepared by third-party industry analysts. SUCH ASSUMPTIONS ARE KEY FACTORS UPON WHICH THE FINANCIAL RESULTS OF THE PICTURE DEPEND. SOME ASSUMPTIONS MAY NOT MATERIALIZE AND UNANTICIPATED EVENTS AND CIRCUMSTANCES MAY OCCUR SUBSEQUENT TO THE DATE OF THESE PROJECTIONS. THEREFORE, THE ACTUAL RESULTS ACHIEVED DURING THE PROJECTION PERIOD MAY VARY FROM SUCH PROJECTIONS AND THE VARIATIONS MAY BE MATERIAL (SEE "SAMPLE REVENUE PROJECTIONS" AT EXHIBIT "D").

NO REPRESENTATION OR WARRANTY IS TO BE INFERRED FROM SUCH PROJECTIONS. INVESTORS ARE URGED, THEREFORE, TO CONSULT THEIR OWN ADVISOR (WHOSE VIEWS MAY DIFFER FROM THOSE DESCRIBED IN THESE PROJECTIONS WITH RESPECT TO THE STATED ASSUMPTIONS OR PROJECTED NUMBERS). SPECIFICALLY, THE ASSUMPTIONS AND PROJECTIONS REGARDING THE AMOUNT AND TIMING OF DISTRIBUTIONS TO INVESTOR/MEMBERS MUST BE CONSIDERED OBJECTIVES. NO ASSURANCES CAN BE PROVIDED THAT SUCH OBJECTIVES WILL BE MET. THE "RISK FACTORS" SECTION OF THIS BUSINESS PLAN IS AN INTEGRAL PART OF THE SAMPLE REVENUE PROJECTIONS.

10. Financial Projections

Financial projections are estimates of the future economic performance of a proposed business or venture. Financial projections are not required for investor offerings for film projects regardless of whether the selected investment vehicle involves the sale to a few active investors in a nonsecurities transaction or the sale of securities to a larger group of passive investors. However, investors seem to prefer that a presentation of financial projections accompany whatever documentation is used to approach such investors. Financial projections provide the prospective investor and the film producer seeking investor financing with an additional point of discussion, and these projections certainly serve as an excellent exercise for the producer in helping him or her to understand how film revenues might flow back to the financing vehicle, the producer group and the investors. In all likelihood, a producer seeking investor financing will be subjected to questions from investors about how they will get their money back and make a profit, and, thus, it behooves the producer to do some research about this aspect of the transaction, to understand it and to be able to explain it as clearly as possible.

Some entertainment attorneys claim that including financial projections with a business plan (or PPM for that matter) will inevitably result in a lawsuit, but it really depends on how well the financial projections are drafted. Also, in contrast to statements by some business-plan consultants, the point of financial projections is not to show investors how profitable the filmmaker's business will be. Use of the word "will" in the context of financial projections is reckless. Instead, the purpose of financial projections is to show how the revenues may flow back to the investor in the event the assumptions upon which the financial projections are based come to fruition. In truth, it is very unlikely that all of the many assumptions that have to be made in order to come up with financial projections will turn out to be on target. So, the parties involved are really dealing with good faith estimates in this situation. The best the filmmaker can do is to make his or her assumptions reasonable based on known marketplace conditions and to disclose those assumptions to his or her prospective investors so that everyone knows how the calculations were determined.

If the sale of a security was involved, the SEC actually has a stated position on financial projections and offers some guidelines for their preparation and use. Although, again, not directly applicable to a business plan seeking a few active investors, these SEC guidelines may be helpful in the preparation of financial projections for both nonsecurities (for which a business plan may be used) and private securities offerings (for which a PPM may be used).

Pursuant to SEC regulations,[1] the SEC encourages the use of management's projections of future economic performance that have a reasonable basis and are presented in an appropriate format. As noted above, this means, among other things, that financial projections are not required for securities disclosure documents and, again reasoning by analogy, are not legally required for business plans. Most business plan consultants strongly urge business-plan preparers to include financial projections—possibly because investors like to see them. From the SEC's perspective, the following guidelines set forth the commission's views on important factors to consider in preparing and disclosing financial projections.

Basis for projections. A film producer (i.e., management) has the option to present its good faith assessment of a small business issuer's future performance. The term "issuer" is securities terminology for the company or investment vehicle that is issuing the securities. For purposes of a business plan used with active investors in a nonsecurities transaction, that would correspond to the company, production company or investment vehicle selling the shares or units in an active-investor investment vehicle.

Such a person or management, however, must have a reasonable basis for such an assessment. In other words, the calculations and numbers associated with financial projections must be based on assumptions, and those assumptions must be reasonable in light of current circumstances in the industry. Such assumptions cannot represent wild speculation on the part of the producer regarding the anticipated earnings of a proposed film (see the sample assumptions associated with the sample financial projections below). These assumptions are narrative statements regarding the many options or decisions that will have to be made in the future as the project proceeds. In other words, a filmmaker assumes certain things will happen for purposes of preparing the financial projections.

The use of unreasonable financial projections is often cited as one of the more important and common mistakes made in the preparation of business plans. The assumptions used as the basis of the financial projections will need to be developed through the filmmaker's own knowledge of the industry and any additional research required. In the alternative, the filmmaker may want to hire a third-party consultant with expertise in the preparation of financial projections for films to aid in the process.

Outside review. An outside review of the film producer's (management's) projections may furnish additional support for the projected results. If a film producer (management) decides to include a report of such a review, it should also disclose the qualifications of the reviewer (per the SEC), the extent of the review, the relationship between the reviewer and the issuer (the filmmaker group) and other material factors concerning the process by which any outside review was sought or obtained. For business-plan preparers, this means it is a good idea to disclose the same or similar biographical information relating to a preparer of financial projections to be used with a film business plan when such financial projections are prepared by a consultant not otherwise affiliated with the filmmaker.

Of course, another one of the disadvantages for a filmmaker using an outside party to review or prepare the financial projections for a film project is that it is less likely that the filmmaker will understand the projections and be able to explain them clearly to investors or answer all of their questions. That can certainly raise doubts in the mind of a prospective investor about the capabilities of the filmmaker and his or her team, the same team that is seeking to persuade prospective investors to invest in the deal. This makes it extremely important that if the filmmaker's team relies on an outside consultant to prepare the financial projections, they need to thoroughly analyze the material prepared by the outside consultant and develop a very good working understanding with respect to how the calculations were made.

On the other hand, these outside consultants will seldom lay out all of their assumptions, for fear that others will borrow their assumptions and prepare their own financial projections, and the consultant may lose out on some future business. This tendency of business-plan consultants flies in the face of the concept of stating the assumptions on which the financial projections are based, since the idea is to make it clear to prospective investors how the calculations of the financial projections were derived. For this reason, if outside consultants are used in the preparation of financial projections for a film, the producers need to urge the preparer of the financial projections to be as forthcoming as possible with respect to clearly laying out all of the assumptions upon which the calculations are based. It may be a good idea to set out that requirement in the contract between the producer group and the preparer of the financial projections before the work actually starts.

The alternative approach is to have someone on the filmmaker's team actually prepare the financial projections (i.e., physically prepare the financial projections on their own computers). They then can simply use whatever outside expertise or assistance is available from business-plan consultants, accountants, entertainment attorneys or others so that the filmmaker team member actually preparing the financial projections will, it is hoped, gain a better understanding of how the calculations were made. In turn, that puts the preparer of the financial projections in a better position to teach the rest of the filmmaker team members so they all can more effectively communicate with the prospective investors. Presumably, such a person would not have the same conflict as the outside consultant who prepares financial projections and does not want to share all of the assumptions used.

Format for projections. Traditionally, projections have been given for three financial items generally considered to be of primary importance to investors [revenues, net income (loss) and earnings (loss) per share or unit], however, projection information need not necessarily be limited to these three items. Again, the issue of long-term corporate finance versus shorter- or limited-term project financing may influence the choice of financial items to project.

Further, a producer (management) should take care to assure that the choice of items projected is not susceptible to misleading inferences through selective projection of only favorable items. It generally would be misleading to present sales or revenue projections without also disclosing various types of income. In the context of a film offering, one of the assumptions upon which the financial projections are based might include the average domestic box-office performances of similar films that have already been released. Such an average may be based on the performance information already presented in the box-office-comparables section of the business plan.

Period covered. The period that appropriately may be covered by the financial projections depends to a large extent on the particular circumstances of the company involved. For certain companies in certain industries, a projection covering a two- or three-year period may be entirely reasonable. Other companies or business ventures may not have a reasonable basis for projections beyond the current year. For a film project, attempting to annualize (project expenses and revenues for each year) may create an unnecessary quagmire of information that cannot be understood by either the prospective investors or the producer. A simpler presentation would involve the financial results of exploiting the film in all markets and media after a stated number of years (e.g., seven years).

Investor understanding. Disclosures accompanying the projections should facilitate investor understanding of the basis for and limitations of the financial projections. The SEC believes that investor understanding would be enhanced by disclosure of the assumptions that in management's opinion are most significant to the projections or are the key factors upon which the financial results of the enterprise depend. The SEC thus encourages disclosure of assumptions in a manner that will provide a framework for analysis of the projections. In other words, the assumptions on which the calculations and numbers are based not only should be reasonable, based on what is currently occurring in the industry, but they should be set forth in writing (i.e., fully disclosed).

With the ideal of investor understanding in mind and recognizing that it is impossible to predict with any accuracy how any independent feature or documentary film may perform in the marketplace, it would appear to be even more safe to offer several sets of calculations (e.g., using a three-column format to show "Poor Performance," "Good Performance" and "Excellent Performance"). That way, it is clear to prospective investors that the film producer, or whoever prepared the financial projections, is not attempting to predict the future performance of the film. Instead, he or she is simply illustrating how the film's revenues may flow back to the investors and what deductions may be taken from the revenue stream at various stages along the way, while basing the projections on certain reasonable and written assumptions that accompany the actual numbers and calculations. This makes the transaction transparent.

The amount of detail. Some film producers (or outside consultants who prepare financial projections) often make the mistake of trying to provide too much detail with respect to anticipated revenue streams when preparing financial projections associated with investor financing of a film project. In many such instances, neither the producer nor the prospective investors understand such complicated projections, and the money paid for them to outside consultants may be wasted. In any case, such elaborate projections do not come any closer to accurately projecting the financial results of a film project than the format recommended here. In addition, the film industry is notorious for failing to provide useful, relevant and accurate financial information regarding the prior performances of feature films, even more so for the markets and media beyond the theatrical marketplace and worse yet for the independent sector. For that reason, it may be a lost cause to attempt to find reliable information regarding anticipated revenues from each of the individual markets and media through which a film might generate income, certainly not without expending significant amounts of money on subscriptions and fees paid to proprietary publications. Merely assuming a reasonable overall-performance level for a film possibly based on the average taken from the earlier reported box-office comparables for your film (as it is exploited in all markets and media throughout the world) and then deducting the expected (and reasonable) fees, expenses and percentage participations from the revenue stream as it flows back to the investor group may be a more rational approach. Even so, such an approach is a compromise attempting to balance the reasonable information needs of the prospective investor with the realities of the marketplace.

Return on investment. Another problem often appearing in the film financial projections prepared by outside consultants, certainly for business plans that have not yet committed to a specific investment vehicle and revenue-sharing deal as between the producer group and the prospective investors, is that such deferred decisions make it impossible for the preparer of the financial projections to carry the calculations all the way out to the return on investment (ROI) for an individual. That is why financial projections prepared by outside consultants often stop at the producer level. In other words, they show how much money may be returned to the producer group but fall short of disclosing how the investors may benefit.

Normally, investors want to know what percentage of their original invested capital is likely to be returned to them and the greater the percentage, the better. For investors, that may be one of the most important reasons for preparing financial projections.

The ROI is the percentage profit that the investor made, not the amount of money the investor got back, that is, the ROI is the amount of money the investor got back after the original investment has been repaid). The ROI is displayed as a percentage of the original investment. Assuming a member-managed LLC is the investment vehicle, the ROI is the earnings per LLC unit divided by the amount the investor put in, then multiplied by 100 to convert the result into a percentage.

In order for anyone to calculate the return on investment from the investor's point of view, that person would have to know whether a certain amount of the investment vehicle's gross revenues may be used by the investment vehicle for its operating costs (along with a corresponding reasonable assumption), what the initial revenue-sharing ratio between the producer group and the investor group is and whether that revenue-sharing ratio changes after some level of priority recoupment for the investor group. Without those decisions being made and disclosed in the business plan, the preparer of the associated financial projections is forced to stop the calculations at that stage of the revenue stream received by the producer group. That approach, of course, leaves the investors wondering how the division of revenues is going to proceed from the producer to the investor group, not really a helpful selling point with prospective investors.

Sample "Film Financial Projections"
Financial Projections for the movie "Snowbound"
ASSUMPTIONS FOR FINANCIAL PROJECTIONS

The following projections estimate several possible revenue streams that may flow back to investors based on three stated distributor-gross-receipts scenarios. These projections serve only as a guide for investors who would like to estimate their possible return based on different scenarios. The numerous variables in feature film distribution cannot be predicted in advance with certainty.

Therefore, there is no way to determine in advance the distribution path or success of the Film *Snowbound*, and of course, there is no guarantee that any particular film will be able to obtain a distribution deal at all.

The accompanying financial projections assume that:

1. The Snowbound Film Production LLC was successful in raising $500,000 from 2 active investors, at $250,000 per LLC unit (2 Units in the member-managed LLC).

2. The film was completed and was of a quality to be of interest to distributors.

3. The producers were successful in obtaining distributor interest and negotiating a single distribution deal for worldwide rights and a theatrical release without the assistance of a producer's representative (thus no fee is deducted for a producer's rep).

4. The distributor did not purchase the film outright but licensed worldwide rights to distribute the film, and the distributor agreed to a $1,000,000 producer's advance recoupable out of the distributor's gross receipts.

5. The lowest average domestic box-office gross for the extensive listing of comparable films represented in tables 1 through 6 on pages 55–59 of the main body of the accompanying Business Plan for various forms of independent films released in the period 1995 through 2008 is $1,027,477. For purposes of these calculations, that number has been assumed as the domestic box-office gross for the "Poor Performance" column in table 10.1.

The average domestic box-office gross in the above-cited Box Office Comparables section of the Business Plan is $4,722,243. For purposes of these calculations, that number has been assumed as the worldwide box-office gross for the "Good Performance" column in table 10.1. Note that it would have been reasonable to assume a higher domestic box-office-gross number for the "Excellent Performance" column, but for purposes of these financial projections, several high-performing films, which could be considered more the exception than the rule, were left out of the average box-office comparables to create a more conservative assumed domestic box-office gross for the "Excellent Performance" column of $15,856,444.

6. The split between domestic and international revenues is assumed to be 48 percent and 52 percent. In other words, for every $48 dollars the movie makes at the domestic box office, it makes $52 dollars at the international box office. Mathematically, that may be stated as:

$$\frac{IBO}{DBO} = \frac{52}{48}$$

Given DBO, calculating IBO is by cross multiplication. So $48 \times IBO = 52 \times DBO$. Then both sides of the equation are divided by 48 to get IBO by itself.

7. In each column, the distributor's share (distributor rentals) of the film's worldwide box-office gross is assumed to be equal to 43 percent of the box-office total. Thus, once the domestic box-office number and the international box-office number are added to arrive at the worldwide box-office number, 43 percent of that

worldwide box-office number may be added to the distributor's gross receipts as distributor rentals (i.e., the distributor's share of the film box office).

8. The percentages of distributor gross receipts attributed to each market and media are assumed to be fairly consistent with the Paul Kagan Associates media studies relating to distributor revenue streams as reported in the main body of the Business Plan on pages 21 and 22. Note that the distributor rental numbers and the numbers for domestic and international ancillary revenues represent the gross receipts received by the distributor, as opposed to any form of domestic, international or worldwide gross. Thus, distributor rentals accounts for 22 percent of the distributor's gross receipts, and ancillary revenues account for 78 percent of the distributor's gross receipts (split 38 percent for the domestic ancillary and 40 percent for the international).

9. The distributor's gross receipts at the end of a seven-year period of exploitation for the film in all markets and media equal the three different levels shown as "Poor Performance," "Good Performance" and "Excellent Performance," and the primary revenue streams are as shown. These distributor-gross-receipts numbers are determined in the following manner. Since distributor rentals represent approximately 22 percent of the distributor's gross receipts (per the Paul Kagan Associates' chart) distributor's gross receipts (DGR) = (100 ÷ 22) multiplied by the distributor rental (DR) number in each column.

10. The distributor's fee is assumed to be an average of 40 percent across the board (not a real-world average since the distributor may apply a different percentage for its fee in each market and media).

11. Since the distributor advanced $1,000,000 to the production company but later recouped that same $1,000,000 out of the film's revenue stream, that transaction does not have to be shown in these financial projections.

12. The distributor's recoupable distribution expenses for the film's theatrical release are assumed to be the three slightly varying amounts shown. Note there is no particular percentage relationship between the Film's assumed distributor expenses and the film's budget.

13. The LLC/production company's negotiated share of the film's net profits is assumed to be 50 percent.

14. The LLC is authorized to make specified deductions from the LLC's gross revenues as per the LLC's definition of LLC Distributable Cash, but such deductions are likely to be relatively minimal, thus such deductions are not calculated for purposes of generating these financial projections.

15. The accumulated LLC Distributable Cash (i.e., net revenues to the LLC) equals the amounts shown in each column.

16. The portion of the LLC's Distributable Cash first paid to the investor group as their priority recoupment is 100 percent, and investor recoupment is defined as 100 percent of the LLC investors' original invested capital as per the LLC

Operating Agreement and Business Plan (for purposes of these calculations, assumed to be $500,000). Since, as noted above, the distributor is assumed to have advanced $1,000,000 to the production company as a recoupable advance and then recouped that advance out of the Film's revenue stream before investor recoupment, that transaction is a wash for purposes of these calculations, and investor recoupment can be assumed to be the full 100 percent or $500,000.

Table 10.1.
Financial projections for Snowbound Productions LLC

Revenue sources and deductions	Performance		
	Poor	Good	Excellent
Domestic box-office gross	1,027,477	4,722,243	15,856,444
International box-office gross	1,297,034	5,961,119	20,016,365
Worldwide box-office gross	2,324,511	10,683,362	35,872,809
Distributor rentals[1]	999,540	4,593,846	15,425,308
Ancillary[2]			
Domestic ancillary	1,853,038	8,516,493	28,596,852
International ancillary	1,959,915	9,007,695	30,246,221
Distributor gross receipts[3]	4,812,493	22,118,034	74,268,381
Distributor fees (40%)	(1,924,997)	(8,847,214)	(29,707,352)
Distribution expenses	(500,000)	(2,000,000)	(8,000,000)
Film's net profits	2,387,496	11,270,820	36,561,029
LLC's share of net profits	1,193,748	5,635,410	18,280,514
Investor recoupment	(250,000)	(250,000)	(250,000)
Creative deferments	0	0	0
Postrecoupment distributable cash	943,748	5,385,410	18,030,514
Investor share (50%)	471,874	2,692,705	9,015,257
Earnings per LLC unit	235,937	1,346,352	4,507,628
Projected ROI	94.37%	538.54%	1,803.05%

NOTES. 1. The term "Distributor rentals" refers to that portion of a film's box-office gross that is remitted to the distributor for the film's theatrical release only.

2. The ancillary marketplace is defined for these purposes to refer to the markets and media in which the film is exploited other than the theatrical marketplace. Thus, ancillary includes home video/DVD, network television, pay television, syndicated television, basic cable, merchandising/licensing, pay-per-view (PPV), direct broadcast satellite (DBS), near video on demand/video on demand (NVOD/VOD), digital streaming and direct-to-theater delivery, hotel, airline, military and other. However, the numbers shown here represent that portion of the distributor's gross receipts attributed to the ancillary marketplace, not the film's worldwide ancillary gross.

3. The term "Distributor gross receipts" includes all revenues received by the distributor for the exploitation of the film in all markets and media.

17. The financial projections further assume that no creative deferments were paid to specified creative personnel after investor recoupment.

18. The revenue-sharing ratio as between the LLC's original member-managers (the producer group) and the other LLC member-managers (the cash investors) is assumed to have changed to 50/50 (as per the LLC Operating Agreement and Business Plan) after the cash investors have recouped as defined above.

19. The earnings or loss per LLC Unit is as shown in each of the three columns.

20. The percentage return on investment (ROI) is projected as shown for each column. Note that at this point in the Film's revenue stream, the Investors have already recouped their original capital investment of $500,000, thus in laymen's terms, the ROI is the percentage profit that the investor made, not the amount of money the investor got back (i.e., the ROI is the amount of money the investor got back after the original investment has been repaid). The ROI is displayed as a percentage of the original investment. In other words, ROI is the earnings per LLC unit divided by the amount the investor put in (for purposes of these calculations the price of a single unit, or $250,000), then multiplied by 100 to turn it into a percentage.

11. Risk Factors

Some business-plan consultants state that a "Risk Factors" section is required for a business plan. That is not true. A "Risk Factors" section is required for a securities disclosure document, and it is even required to appear in the "forepart" of that securities disclosure document, but there is no one with the authority to impose such a requirement on a business plan. Others may take the more moderated and accurate position that a "Risk Factors" section in a business plan is still a good idea, and that's ok. It's a good idea because it cautions investors in advance that there a number of specific risk factors involved in the proposed investment, and, thus, such investors are less likely to complain later that the filmmaker did not advise them of such risks.

On the other hand, the risk factors section is quite negative and if actually read by a filmmaker's prospective investors, it may discourage them from investing. In any case, if a filmmaker chooses to include a risk factors section in his or her business plan, he or she should not succumb to the temptation of watering down the risks or including his or her arguments against or plans to mollify the risks in that same section. The filmmaker should just state the risk factors in the "Risk Factors" section and use the rest of the business plan to show the investors how he or she hopes to reduce or avoid such risks.

If again the securities laws serve as a guide as to what a "Risk Factors" section ought to include, here is what the SEC's Regulation S-B says about risk factors at Item 503. The risk factors section ought to include a discussion of "any factors that make the offering speculative or risky." Those factors, modified slightly to work with a business plan, may include, among other things, the following:

1. The lack of an operating history
2. The lack of recent profits from operations
3. The company's poor financial position

4. Risks associated with the business or proposed business

5. The lack of a market for the shares or units being sold

Again, these same securities rules state where the risk-factors section must appear: "The risk factor discussion must immediately follow the summary section. If you do not include a summary section, the risk factor discussion must immediately follow the cover page." Once again, however, SEC rules do not apply to business plans, thus it may be presumed that if a "Risk Factors" section is to be included in a film business plan, it may be placed wherever the filmmaker chooses. [Note. These sample risk factors are for a development deal, not a production offering.]

Sample "Risk Factors"
Risk Factors

Investment in the LLC involves various risks relating both to the nature of the financing vehicle (a member-managed limited-liability company) and the movie industry itself, and such investment is therefore suitable only for persons or entities with the financial capability of making and holding long-term investments. Prospective Purchasers should consider the following factors, among others, before making a decision to purchase interests:

LLC RISKS

1. Development stage company. The LLC will be a newly organized company with minimal assets and no history of operations. The LLC is being formed specifically for the purpose of financing the acquisition, development, packaging and promotion for production financing of a single motion-picture project. Although there are significant risks in the development, production and distribution of films generally, the LLC is subject to the general risks inherent in the establishment of a new business venture, including the absence of an operating history.

2. Lack of management experience. The original Member-Manager of the LLC (Larry Cawley) has limited experience in relation to managing the affairs of an LLC. The LLC's success may depend in large part upon the services provided by other individuals not employed by the LLC.

3. Reliance on management. No assurances can be provided that the LLC's management will perform adequately or that LLC operations will be successful. In particular, the LLC will depend on the services of the individual Larry Cawley, along with others associated with the LLC (see "Description of Business—People of the XYZ Film Production LLC" and "LLC Management"). Unit Holders will all participate in the management of the LLC. All decisions with respect to the management of the LLC will be made exclusively by its Member-Managers. Accordingly, no person should purchase any of the Units offered hereby unless such

Prospective Purchaser is willing to entrust all aspects of the management of the LLC to the Member-Manager group as a whole and has evaluated the capabilities of the Member-Managers to perform such functions.

4. *Conflicts of interest.* The Member-Managers are not required to render exclusive services in connection with the Film Project or the LLC. Consequently, the Member-Managers may render services in connection with other business projects, including entertainment projects, during any or all phases of development, production or distribution of the Film Project. The Member-Managers will be required to use their discretion in determining how to allocate time and attention among various ongoing film projects. In addition, each of the Member-Managers may serve in the same positions for other feature film offerings in the future.

5. *No key-man life insurance.* As noted above, the LLC will be relying on the management skills of the individual Member-Managers and others associated with them. However, the LLC has not and does not anticipate purchasing so-called key-man insurance coverage to compensate the LLC in the event that an unexpected loss of the services of such persons occurs. Consequently, the impact of such a loss on the LLC and its efforts to develop and seek production financing for its Film Project may be significant.

6. *Limited transferability.* It is not anticipated that a public trading market will develop for the Units offered hereby. Neither the LLC nor the Member-Managers are obligated to redeem or repurchase any of the LLC Units. Unit Holders may not, therefore, be able to liquidate their investments in the event of an emergency. In other words, the Investor must be able to bear the economic risk of maintaining an investment in the LLC for the life of the LLC, which may be as long as ten (10) years from the date of its formation. In addition, Units may not be accepted as collateral for loans. Also, the Member-Managers may not permit an assignee of Units to become a substituted Member-Manager. Consequently, the purchase of Units should be considered only as a long-term investment.

7. *Decisions by committee.* The Operating Agreement provides that no Member-Manager or Unit Purchaser shall be personally liable for any of the debts, contracts or other obligations of the LLC or for any losses thereof, beyond the amount subscribed for by each Member-Manager in the LLC plus such Member-Manager's share of the undistributed LLC income. The Operating Agreement further provides that the Member-Managers and Unit Purchasers will have the right to take part in the control of the business of the LLC (see "Operating Agreement"). Thus, to a certain extent, all LLC Member-Managers will be actively involved in the important decisions to be made regarding all aspects of the project. Such a decision-making approach may or may not result in the best decisions being made.

8. *Funds to be held in a segregated account.* The Offering proceeds generated by this Offering will be held in a segregated, interest-bearing bank account until the earlier of achieving the Minimum Offering of $500,000 or termination of

the Offering. In the event that this Offering fails to achieve the Minimum, the Offering proceeds will be returned to Investors with interest.

9. *Investor last in line.* A motion picture typically goes from the production/ development company to the distributor, who in turn may send it to territorial subdistributors, who send it to theatrical exhibitors. A negotiated portion of these box-office receipts generated by a motion picture travel this same route in reverse. The exhibitor takes a cut and sends the balance to the subdistributor, who takes a cut and sends the balance to the distributor, who takes a cut and sends the balance to the producer. Except for the possibility that certain fully developed and packaged film projects may be sold outright, the problem for the private investors with this system is that such investors, who have had their money at risk for the longest time, are at the tail end of the box-office-receipts chain, as well as at the end of the chain in regards to other revenues. Thus, if the LLC or subsequent production entity in negotiating a distribution deal has to rely heavily on a participation in some level of the Film's revenue stream to be defined at a later date (which date and level of participation may not be in the LLC's control), revenues to the LLC and thus Purchasers of Units are likely to be the last in line to benefit from such a revenue stream, if any. In addition, of course, LLC investors cannot expect any cash distributions during the development phase of the Film Project, and no assurances can be provided that the LLC will be successful in generating any revenues from any production or distribution efforts; thus, the investors may suffer a loss of their entire investments.

10. *Indemnification provisions may impair LLC.* The Operating Agreement provides that under certain circumstances the Member-Managers, their Affiliates, Counsel and consultants may be indemnified by the LLC for liabilities or losses arising out of such LLC activities in connection with the Film. Should the LLC be required to pay damages or claims pursuant to such indemnification provisions, such payment could reduce or deplete the assets of the LLC.

11. *Possible tax consequences of investment.* In evaluating the purchase of Units as an investment, a Prospective Purchaser should consider the tax risks thereof, including (i) the possible reallocation of net income and net loss and credits; (ii) the tax liability resulting from a sale or other disposition of such Purchaser's Units, or a sale or other disposition of the Film Project, including income, a portion of which may be taxed at ordinary income rates; (iii) the risk that the LLC will be treated as an association taxable as a corporation for federal income-tax purposes; (iv) the possibility that the deductions taken by the LLC in a taxable year might not be allowed in such year or that certain expenses may be required to be capitalized; (v) the possibility that an audit of the LLC's information returns may result in the disallowance of the LLC's deductions and in an audit of such Purchaser's tax return; (vi) recognition that the Member-Managers will have no interest in LLC losses and tax deductions until after the Member-Manager's

capital accounts have been reduced to zero; and (vii) possible adverse changes in the tax laws and their interpretation. All of the above possible tax consequences may result in an increased tax liability for LLC Investors or a reduction in anticipated deductions. In addition, there is a risk that a Purchaser's tax liability may exceed such Purchaser's share of cash distributions for a particular tax year possibly resulting in an out-of-pocket expense for the Purchaser above and beyond any distributions from the LLC. Prospective investors should seek the advice and counsel of their own tax advisers.

Movie-Industry Risks

Some of the development phase activities of the LLC may naturally lead to or overlap with certain preproduction activities for the Film, and certain of the risks associated with a film development offering are similar to risks associated with a production offering since the Film Project is being developed for the purpose of being produced and distributed.

1. *No production financing or distribution is currently in place.* The profitable production and distribution of a motion picture depends in large part on the availability of one or more capable and efficient production companies and distributors who are able to arrange for appropriate production financing, advertising and promotion, proper release dates and bookings in first-run and other theaters. There can be no assurances that profitable production and distribution arrangements will be obtained for the Script or that the Film produced, if produced, can or will be distributed profitably.

2. *The project is long-term.* The development, production and distribution of a motion picture involves the passage of a significant amount of time. Development activities with respect to a motion-picture script may take many months. Preproduction on a picture may extend for two to three months or more. Principal photography may extend for several weeks or more. Postproduction may extend from three to four months or more. Distribution and exhibition of motion pictures generally and of the LLC's Film Project may continue for years before LLC Gross Revenues or Distributable Cash may be generated, if at all.

3. *Development and production activities may be difficult.* Particularly as developed and produced by independent filmmakers, each motion picture is a separate business venture with its own management, employees and equipment and its own budgetary requirements. There are substantial risks associated with film production, including death or disability of key personnel, other factors causing delays, destruction or malfunction of sets or equipment, the inability of production personnel to comply with budgetary or scheduling requirements and physical destruction or damage to the film itself. Significant difficulties such as these may materially increase the cost of production.

4. Commercial success is not certain. The literary material and/or Script to be acquired by the LLC has yet to be produced as a feature film and may never be completed as such, or, if produced, the Film may not be commercially acceptable to distributors. In that event, the LLC will not generate any revenues, and no distributions will be made to investors. In addition, many films are released each year that are not commercially successful and fail to recoup their production costs from United States theatrical distribution. Foreign and ancillary markets have, therefore, become increasingly important. Although both foreign and ancillary markets have grown, neither provides a guarantee of revenue. Licensing of a motion picture in the ancillary markets is particularly dependent upon performance in domestic theatrical distribution. If a motion picture is not an artistic or critical success or if, for any reason, it is not well received by the public, it may be a financial failure.

5. Development or production may be prematurely abandoned. The development, production or distribution of the LLC's Film Project may be abandoned at any stage if further expenditures do not appear commercially feasible, with the resulting loss of some or all of the funds previously expended on their production or distribution, including funds expended in connection with the development and/or preproduction of the Film.

6. Cost overruns may occur. The costs of developing and producing motion pictures can be underestimated and may be increased by reason of factors beyond the control of the producers. Such factors may include weather conditions, illness of technical and artistic personnel, artistic requirements, labor disputes, governmental regulations, equipment breakdowns and other production disruptions. While the LLC intends to engage production personnel who have demonstrated an ability to complete films within the assigned budget, the risk of a film running over budget is always significant and may have a substantial adverse impact on the profitability of the LLC's Film Project.

7. The industry is competitive. Most segments of the motion-picture industry are highly competitive. In both the development and production phases, competition may affect the LLC's ability to obtain the services of preferred writers, performers and other creative personnel. The LLC will be competing with other film development companies in acquiring rights to literary material, in acquiring scripts, hiring development personnel and attaching directors and actors to the LLC's Film Project. Once produced, the Film will be competing for distribution slots in all available markets and media. In the distribution phase, competition may limit the availability of such markets and media required for the successful distribution of the Picture. The Picture will be competing directly with other motion pictures and indirectly with other forms of public entertainment. The LLC will compete with numerous larger motion-picture-production companies and distribution companies that have substantially greater resources, larger and more-experienced production and distribution staff and established histories of successful production and distribution of motion pictures.

8. *The industry is constantly changing.* The entertainment business in general and the motion picture business in particular are undergoing significant changes, primarily due to technological developments. These developments have resulted in the availability of alternative forms of leisure-time entertainment, including expanded pay television, basic cable television, syndicated television, videocassettes, video discs, DVD, video games and the Internet. Revenues from licensing of motion pictures to such media will vary from year to year relative to each other. The level of theatrical success remains a critical factor in generating revenues in these ancillary markets. It is impossible to accurately predict the effect that these and other new technological developments may have on the motion picture industry (see "Motion-Picture-Industry Overview").

9. *Foreign distribution is perilous.* Foreign distribution of a motion picture (i.e., outside the United States and Canada) may require the use of various foreign distributors. Some foreign countries may impose government regulations on the distribution of films. Also revenues derived from the distribution of the Picture in foreign countries, if any, may be subject to currency controls and other restrictions that may temporarily or permanently prevent the inclusion of such revenue in the distributor's gross receipts or the LLC's Gross Revenues.

10. *Audience appeal is unpredictable.* The ultimate profitability of any motion picture depends upon its audience appeal in relation to the cost of its development, production and distribution. The audience appeal of a given motion picture depends, among other things, on unpredictable critical reviews and changing public tastes, and such appeal cannot be anticipated with certainty.

12. Miscellaneous Provisions

In this section, which would typically appear at the end of the main body of the business plan, a filmmaker would include various items of information that might not otherwise be covered in the other sections of the document. Subsections of the "Miscellaneous Provisions" section may include "Reports to Active Investors and Others," "Pending Legal Proceedings" and "Access to Additional Information."

Reports to active investors and others. In this subsection, the filmmaker will want to explain to his or her prospective investors how the filmmaker plans to keep them informed about the progress of the fund-raising activities and the production and distribution of the film. This may include information about the type of communication to be used (e.g., newsletter, e-mail, and the like) and how often the information will be provided. Of course, in any investor-financed business venture, it is extremely important to keep the investors informed.

Pending legal proceedings. In this subsection, the filmmaker will want to make a statement regarding whether he or she is aware of any pending or threatened legal proceedings to which he or she or his or her company is or may be parties to and which may materially affect his or her proposed business activities. This subsection is required for a securities disclosure document, and although not required for a business plan, it is certainly information that prospective investors should know before they decide whether or not to invest. If there is some pending legal proceeding, add a brief summary statement of what is involved and provide the factual information so that prospective investors can find out more if they choose to.

Access to additional information. In this subsection, the filmmaker will want to explain to his or her prospective investors that they should carefully read the business plan and its accompanying exhibits. In addition, he or she will want to advise them that they have the opportunity to ask whatever questions they may have. This subsection will also disclose that investors or their representatives can review the files and records of the business during reasonable business hours and with notice.

Sample "Miscellaneous Provisions"

Miscellaneous Provisions

REPORTS TO ACTIVE INVESTORS AND OTHERS

The Producer will prepare and distribute to any Investor who may participate in the financing of the development and/or production costs associated with the Picture a quarterly report regarding the status of the project including a breakdown on expenditures.

PENDING LEGAL PROCEEDINGS

The Producers are not aware of any pending or threatened legal proceedings to which they or the Production Company or its owners are, or may be parties to, and which is materially relevant to this Business Plan or their participation herein.

ACCESS TO ADDITIONAL INFORMATION

Any prospective Investor is urged to read this Business Plan and the attached Exhibits carefully and to have the documents reviewed by an investment adviser. To the extent possible, the Producer will answer any questions that a prospective Investor may have and will attempt to provide any additional documentation to verify the statements included herein.

The Producer will keep at the principal place of business of the Production Company adequate books of account of the Production Company and for the Picture, and any Investor and his or her authorized representatives will have at all times, during reasonable business hours, free access to and the right to inspect and copy such books of account.

13. Appendixes to the Business Plan

A variety of documents may prove useful as appendices or exhibits to a business plan being used to help raise investor funds for a film project. A general question that may serve as a good guideline for determining whether a document ought to be included as an appendix to the business plan is, "Would the document be important to a prospective investor in deciding whether or not to invest in the venture?" Another counter consideration, however, is whether the document is too long. Examples of documents that may be too long to include as an appendix include the screenplay, which may be better represented in the business plan by a synopsis. Also, the complete budget would be too long. This kind of financial information is typically represented in the business plan with something akin to the top sheet of the film's budget, plus the expenses to be incurred in putting the deal together and raising the money from investors. As noted earlier, these latter two items are not film budget items, so they should be set out separate from the film budget portion of the "Estimated Use of Proceeds" (see discussion in chapter 9).

The appendix to a business plan is a good place to include some charts and graphs, but be sure to include enough narrative explanations with the charts and graphs so that they can be easily understood by readers of the business plan. Charts and graphs that are difficult to decipher are not that useful.

Résumés. In the event that the filmmaker chooses to take the summary approach to the biographies of key people committed to the project (not recommended), he or she may then want to supplement those biographies with the actual résumés of such people. This approach is somewhat redundant because some of the information will appear in both the body of the business plan as well as in the résumé. For that reason, it is preferable to draft a more comprehensive narrative biography to include in the body of the business plan and avoid the duplication in including résumés as an appendix.

Material agreements. Any existing and important agreements that relate to the business and its proposed activity may be included as appendixes to the business plan. For a film project those agreements may include literary-property option agreement, or option/acquisition agreement, life-story rights agreement, screenwriter agreement, producer agreement, director's agreement, director of photography agreement, consultant agreement and/or distribution agreement.[1]

Financial statements. In the event that an existing company is involved, the financial statements relating to its current financial status may be included. Since such financial statements are typically prepared by an outside accountant, it may work best to insert them as an appendix and include just a summary of their report in the "Financial Information" section of the business plan.

Letters of interest or letters of intent. To the extent that the producer has gathered letters of interest or intent from various prospective participants in the development or production of the film, copies of these may be inserted behind a cover page with the heading "Letters of Interest/Intent."[2] Such letters are typically made contingent on certain events such as the project being successfully funded, mutual agreement as to the person's compensation and no other contractual conflicts with the time period in which such person's services will be required. Although some will argue that letters of interest/intent are worthless, these letters at least show that the producer has identified appropriate people to handle certain roles in the production of the film and has contacted those people, and they in turn have read the script (if so) and have expressed an interest in performing the requested services. That's better than not being able to demonstrate any interest at all.

Industry articles. The producer may want to insert behind a cover page with the heading "Industry Articles" copies of several published articles that provide additional information about the industry or segment of the industry being promoted through the business plan. Information coming from a third-party and published source may add some additional credibility to the business plan. Also, some statements that would appear speculative and therefore may not be appropriate to include in the body of the business plan, might not seem so out of place within the context of a published article or when expressed as someone else's opinion.

Press coverage. This appendix may include copies of material written about any of the participants in the project that have appeared in the regular or trade press. Sometimes, the "Industry Articles" and "Press Coverage" appendixes may be combined behind a single cover page called "Industry Articles and Press Coverage."

Financial projections. As a practical matter, this information may be treated as an appendix to the business plan simply because it is often prepared by a third party, who may have used a different format than that of the business plan (see earlier discussion of "Financial Projections").

Investment vehicle agreements. If the business plan is drafted so as to include a specific investment vehicle such as an investor financing agreement or a joint-venture agreement, a copy of such an agreement may be included as an appendix to the main document.[3] If however, such documents are to be signed by the investor and returned to the producer, they should not be included as an exhibit or bound with the business plan. If the investment vehicle is a member-managed LLC, an appropriate exhibit or appendix would be an LLC operating agreement specifically tailored to the needs of a member-managed LLC. Understand that not only are the provisions of a member-managed LLC operating agreement different from the provisions of a manager-managed LLC (so the two cannot be substituted for each other) but also some of the language and provisions of a member-managed LLC may differ somewhat from state to state. Because an LLC is created based on the statutory scheme of a specific state, the member-managed LLC operating agreement must be drafted based on the specific requirements of the selected state.

If the proposed investment vehicle is a corporation to be formed upon funding, a draft of the proposed articles of incorporation to be filed with the secretary of state in the state in which the corporation is to be formed may be included as an appendix to the business plan. Sample shareholder and board of director minutes and/or corporate bylaws may also be included.

Each of the agreements discussed above represents a complicated set of decisions with legal implications. For that reason, it is not advisable for independent-film producers to attempt to draft their own investment vehicle agreements. The services of an attorney familiar with these specific transactions should be obtained.

Other possible appendixes. The following is a brief list of other possible exhibits (depending on the stage at which financing is sought and whether or not already incorporated in the body of the business plan) that may be included as part of the business plan:

title report
copyright search report
chain-of-title documents, including a certificate of authorship for the
    screenplay
copy of the copyright registration
copyright assignment form
completion bond commitment letter (if any)
corporate resolution authorizing the producer to negotiate and sign a
    financing agreement
cast and production credits
script treatment
copies of story board drawings
biographies of key people

feature stories on lead actors and the director
production stills
casual cast photos
agreements relating to the film's music
MPAA ratings certificate (if available)
E&O certificate of insurance
distribution agreement(s)

Note again that the completion bond is also not a form of film finance but merely a financial arrangement that helps facilitate certain film finance transactions. For example, on most lender transactions (i.e., negative pick-ups, foreign presales, gap and supergap financing and the insurance-backed schemes—all forms of lender financing), the banks will always insist that the producer obtain a completion bond to assure that the bank will not have to worry about the film going over budget or not being completed. That is simply a risk that the bank will not assume. Sometimes, the studios will also choose to purchase a completion bond on some of their films, and some independent producers may choose to purchase a completion bond for an investor-financed film. However, the vast majority of the low- and ultralow-budget motion pictures produced by independent producers each year probably do not use a completion bond.

14. Where to Find Investors

One of the most commonly asked questions relating to investor financing of film companies or projects is, "Where can I find prospective investors?" Often, the question is based on one or more false premises. Such a question may assume that investors likely to invest in risky film ventures gather at a particular physical location or that the investors who invest in independent film often return to invest again after their first investment. Neither of these described situations are generally accurate, although occasionally prospective investors might show up at a film-finance seminar seeking to learn more about how film financing works. In such instances, however, these investors may or may not actually reveal who they are or that they are investors. Even if they do reveal their presence, they will typically be mobbed by desperate independent filmmakers, and the experience is not likely to be favorable.

Many independent-film producers often state that they believe they have identified and/or have relationships with one or several wealthy investors who can and may fund the entire cost of their film project. Unfortunately, it rarely happens. Investors with money tend to want to spread their investments among a variety of opportunities. That is one of the most fundamental tenants of wealth preservation or investing—diversification. In addition, wealthy investors tend not to want to place a significant portion of their money into the more risky investments and will more likely only allocate a small portion of their wealth for such projects. And truthfully speaking, few investment opportunities are more risky than an independent feature film. This is another reason why a business plan may not be the best choice for raising money from investors since none of the active-investor investment vehicles legally associated with a business plan offer the opportunity for spreading the risk of the venture among a large group of investors. That's where the passive-investor vehicles and the securities offerings come in. They do allow the film producers to spread the risk of this very risky investment among a large group of passive investors.

In any case, at least one of the keys to or starting points for finding investors (i.e., looking in the right places) is analysis of investor motivation. First, do some brainstorming with associates regarding what might motivate anyone with money to invest some of it in the filmmaker's high-risk venture. Some of the possibilities are listed below. Others may be unique to a specific film project. Some of these descriptions of investor motivation are closely related and may even overlap. They are presented in no particular order.

> *Career support.* A prospective investor has close ties with the filmmaker and is interested in supporting the filmmaker's career.
>
> *Glamour.* An investor is enamored with the glamour of the film industry or the idea of owning a piece of a movie.
>
> *Cocktail chatter.* An investor feels the investment has a certain amount of "cocktail chatter" value (i.e., it's more interesting and fun to talk about than most boring investments in their portfolio).
>
> *Associate.* An investor wants to be able to spend some time on the set and rub elbows with the cast and crew. (This needs to be carefully controlled so that it does not get out of hand and become a distraction.)
>
> *Learning experience.* An investor wants to use this investment as an opportunity to learn about how the film industry works so that he or she can get more involved in the future.
>
> *Extras.* An investor has a son, daughter, niece or nephew who can appear as an extra in the movie.
>
> *Appear in movie.* An investor wants to appear in the movie as an extra or actor or actress in a small part.
>
> *Local economy.* An investor realizes that by investing in the movie, it will help bring the movie to a specific locale that will benefit the local economy.
>
> *Movie message.* An investor is very interested in one or more of the messages being communicated through this significant medium. (All movies communicate something.)
>
> *Tax incentives.* An investor is in a position to take advantage of federal, state or international tax incentives for film-production expenses.
>
> *Screenwriter.* An investor is a screenwriter and wants to get his or her script produced.
>
> *Direct.* An investor is also a director, and (in rare and unusual circumstances) he or she may want to direct the movie, and the filmmaker may be willing to permit that.

Make a profit. Although not usually the sole reason for investing, even investors who invest in films for some of the other reasons may also still hold out hope that such a risky investment will result in a profit.

Approaching investors. Most business-plan consultants advise not to send out unsolicited business plans. Presumably, they will not receive favorable attention. Of course, that approach could also be a huge waste of paper and expense. On the other hand, there are no rules relating to business plan solicitations restricting contact with prospective investors to correspond with the limitations imposed by the SEC for the exempt offerings of securities (i.e., private placements). As a practical matter, however, it may be more acceptable to make an introductory call to inquire of interest, create a Web site that solicits inquiries (the filmmaker needs to make it clear that he or she is only seeking a few active investors), send out a highlights page (i.e., a one-page summary of the offering using bullet points), the business plan's executive summary and/or an introductory letter or e-mail.

This solicitation of prospective investors issue relates to the previously discussed question of whether to specifically disclose in the business plan what investment vehicle is to be used or contemplated as opposed to leaving that question unaddressed and open to negotiation. One of the negatives for taking the approach of not discussing the investment vehicle is that if the business plan comes to the attention of a state or federal securities regulator (someone may receive the solicitation of interest and contact the regulator), the securities regulator may take the position that the filmmaker is selling a security (if it is not clear on the face of the document that this is not the case) and issue a cease-and-desist order demanding that the filmmaker stop the solicitation. This has happened. That's one good reason for the filmmaker to choose a preferred investment vehicle and make sure it is one of the four active-investor investment vehicles discussed in this book. It is equally important to be certain that the language used throughout the business plan and in all prospective investor communications is consistent with the concept of one or a few active investors (i.e., not stating, suggesting or implying at any level that as a result of the filmmaker's rather general solicitation, he or she may accept investments from passive investors).

One of the ways securities regulators sometimes check on this is to call up the producer (i.e., a potential issuer of a security) who is advertising. Pretending to be a prospective investor, the regulator might ask, "What is the smallest size investment you will accept?" If the filmmaker says $5,000, when he or she is trying to raise $1 million or some other high number, that makes it clear that the filmmaker anticipates or may accept investments from such a large number of investors that it will be virtually impossible for all of them to be active. If one or more of the investors are passive, the filmmaker has sold a security, no matter what he or she thinks it is or calls it. Thus again, to be safe, it is best to be clear throughout the business plan and in all prospective investor communications that a security is not being sold, not by just providing one or more statements in capital letters (a disclaimer) but by actually choosing the right investment vehicle and keeping all language throughout the document and in conversations with prospective investors consistent with the active-investor concept.

Copying and binding suggestions. Copy shops offer a variety of binding options, which include spiral binding, tape binding, VeloBind, perfect binding and so forth. When the business plan is ready, the filmmaker should check several copy shops for the best price, usually offered on a per-page basis. Discuss the various binding choices with the copy shop's personnel. Color, of course, is more expensive than black and white. Copying front and back saves paper and money. Because the beginning page of each major section should start on the right side (odd-numbered pages) of the document, the preparers of business plans often insert the statement "(This Page Left Blank Intentionally)" on even-numbered pages without any text. As a final check of the document while it is still in the computer, cursor through to see that each beginning page of a major section falls on an odd-numbered page, and if not, insert a page break for a blank, even-numbered page and add "(This Page Left Blank Intentionally)."

As noted earlier, business-plan covers for film projects often feature some form of art work or graphic design. This is an opportunity for some color to create a bit of pop for the business plan that may separate it from other more mundane offerings.

Conclusion

The most accurate statement to make about using a business plan to seek film financing is to say that it may be used with an appropriate active-investor investment vehicle to raise money from active investors. However, the federal courts interpreting SEC regulations have narrowed the definition of active investors to those with "knowledge and experience" in the relevant industry (in this case, the film industry).[1]

Thus, independent producers seeking to raise money from people outside the film industry who have little to no knowledge of the film industry and no experience working in the film industry simply do not qualify as active investors. For that reason, a business plan cannot legally be used as the sole document to provide information to such prospective investors.

Business plans are not adequate to provide information to passive investors (that requires a properly drafted securities disclosure document because a security is being offered).

A business plan is not needed to seek investment from one, two or three active investors from within the film industry (i.e., people with knowledge and experience in the subject industry who are still working in the industry) because they generally do not need to see a business plan—a producer's package is enough. An independent producer would likely appear to be somewhat amateurish to offer a business plan to a prospective active investor who has knowledge of and experience in the film industry and still works in the industry. Further, people or companies in the film industry do not typically want to be investors. They are more inclined to want to own or control the project.

Also, the business plan is not very useful in obtaining production-money loans for a film. Most production loans in the film industry are backed by distribution agreements and guarantees provided by credit-worthy distributors, and a business plan is not needed to approach such distributors. Again, the producer's package is adequate. A business plan may be helpful in approaching a bank seeking a loan backed by other collateral (e.g., the independent producer's house), but that has never really been a good idea for risky film deals, unless the filmmaker is willing to lose the house.

Thus, in all fairness and in direct contravention to what many business-plan consultants have been telling independent filmmakers for years, a business plan is far less useful in the film business than most people think. An independent producer may feel that creating such a business plan is useful as a planning tool or may be willing to accept significant involvement of a few active investors.

Maybe this book will come to the attention of business-plan consultants around the country, and they can bring their advice about the usefulness of business plans into compliance with the law. It clearly appears that many business-plan consultants are not aware of the limitations on active investors imposed by the law and are overselling the usefulness of the business plan to unsuspecting filmmakers who are trying to deal with prospective investors. If a consultant does not agree with the law, then he or she should seek to change such laws in a legitimate manner rather than ignoring the law and risking the finances and futures of their clients and themselves.

The good news, again, is that a business plan is the appropriate informational document with which to approach one or a few active investors who have knowledge and experience in the film industry, so long as it is or can be accompanied by an appropriate active-investor investment vehicle, and the agreement between the investors and the filmmaker clearly sets out the authority of the active investor or investors to participate in the decision-making process. In addition, a properly drafted generic business plan may also be used to conduct a general solicitation seeking active investors, and if that effort fails, selected contents of the business plan may be converted into a securities disclosure document that may be used to seek passive investors for a private placement. If done properly, the conduct of the general solicitation using the business plan effectively served as an opportunity to expand the pool of prospective investors for the subsequent private placement, since it may have increased the number of prospective investors with whom the film producer now has the required preexisting relationship. Of course, some may also still promote the business plan for mere planning purposes, for aiding an inexperienced securities attorney in drafting a securities disclosure document or for supplementing the use of a PPM, but as discussed earlier, those uses are negligible for film-finance purposes and are associated with certain risks.

NOTES
BIBLIOGRAPHY
INDEX

Notes

Introduction

1. For more information on this topic, see my book *43 Ways to Finance Your Feature Film*. All references to this volume are to the third edition.

2. Ibid.

3. Ibid., chaps. 7, 8 and 9.

4. See chap. 1, "Preliminary Considerations," in the current volume. For more information on this topic, see my book *43 Ways to Finance Your Feature Film*.

1. Preliminary Considerations

1. For more information on this topic, see my book *43 Ways to Finance Your Feature Film*.

2. Prifti, *Securities*, 10–14.

3. *Williamson v. Tucker*.

4. *Consolidated Management Group, LLC v. the California Department of Corporations*.

5. *SEC v. Merchant Capital, LLC*; *Holden v. Hagopian*; and *Williamson v. Tucker*.

6. For a detailed discussion of these active-investor investment vehicles, see my book *43 Ways to Finance Your Feature Film*, chaps. 3 to 6. Samples of an investor-financing agreement and a joint-venture agreement appear in my book *Film Industry Contracts*, 9–24.

7. For a more detailed explanation of this strategy, see my book *43 Ways to Finance Your Feature Film*, 299.

8. For a more detailed discussion of these more specialized forms of film finance, see my book *43 Ways to Finance Your Feature Film*.

9. For more information on net profits, see my book *Feature Film Distribution Deal*, 19–22, 80, 104–5.

10. For a more detailed discussion relating to the advantages and disadvantages of the four listed active-investor investment vehicles, see my book *43 Ways to Finance Your Feature Film*, chaps. 3 to 6.

11. See my article "Hard Money—Legal Liabilities May Arise for Independent Film Producers Who Rely on Contingent Promissory Notes." *Los Angeles Lawyer*, May 2010, 26–32.

4. The Company or Investment Vehicle

1. For a more in-depth discussion of the features of an S corporation, see my book *43 Ways to Finance Your Feature Film*, third edition, 80–94.

6. Market Overview/State of the Industry

1. The Web sites for the Motion Picture Association of America and the National Association of Theatre Owners are www.mpaa.org and http://natoonline.org, respectively.

2. For a more detailed list of such information sources, see my book *Introduction to the Motion Picture Industry*, chap. 4.

7. The Product or the Film Project

1. See my book *Introduction to the Motion Picture Industry*, chap. 3, "Internet Community Devoted to Film."

2. Tulchin, "Selling Your Movie."

3. National Association of Theatre Owners, http://natoonline.org. A fairly extensive list of currently active video and film distributors with online links appears at www.videouniversity.com.

4. Nielsen EDI is at entdata.com.

5. The Web site for Show Biz Data is showbizdata.com.

6. The Web site for Box Office Report is boxofficereport.com.

9. Financial Information

1. For more discussion relating to offering limited-liability protection to prospective investors, see my *43 Ways to Finance Your Feature Film*, 71–72.

2. For an example of an investor financing agreement, see my book *Film Industry Contracts*, 9.

3. For an example of a joint-venture agreement, see my *Film Industry Contracts*, 15.

4. See *Williamson v. Tucker* and *Consolidated Management Group LLC v. the California Department of Corporations*.

10. Financial Projections

1. U.S. Securities and Exchange Commission.

13. Appendixes to the Business Plan

1. Examples of such agreements are in my book *Film Industry Contracts*.

2. A sample letter of intent is in ibid., 39.

3. Examples of an investor financing agreement and a joint-venture agreement are in ibid., 9, 15.

14. Where to Find Investors

1. See earlier discussions of *Williamson v. Tucker* and *Consolidated Management Group v. the California Department of Corporations.*

Bibliography

Abrams, Rhonda. *The Successful Business Plan: Secrets and Strategies*. 4th ed. Boston: Oasis Press, 2003.

Amdur, Meredith. "Powerful Disc Drive—DVD Spending to Vastly Outweigh Box Office." *Variety.com*, June 28, 2004.

———. "Spending on Media Rises—Growth Forecast to Reach $828 Bil by 2007." *Variety.com*, August 10, 2003.

———. "Wal-Mart Crowned DVD King." *Variety*, July 18, 2004.

Anderson, Chris. *The Long Tail: Why the Future of Business Is Selling Less of More*. New York: Hyperion, 2006.

"Arthur Anderson Media and Entertainment Survey." *Hollywood Reporter*, December 26, 2000–January 1, 2001.

Bender, Pennee. Review of *Hearst over Hollywood: Power, Passion, and Propaganda in the Movies*, by Louis Pizzitola. *Harvard Business School's Business History Review* 76, no. 3 (Autumn 2002). http://www.hbs.edu/bhr/archives/bookreviews/76/2002autumnpbender.pdf.

"Blu-ray FAQ." *Blu-ray.com*. http://www.blu-ray.com/faq/#bluray.

Boursaw, Jane Louise. "Film Fatales—Shocking Statistics about Women in the Film Industry." *MovieMaker Magazine*, Winter 2006.

"Box Office Resists Recession." *Variety*, January 4, 2009.

Burstyn v. Wilson, 343 U.S. 495 (1952).

"CEA DVD Player Sales." *The Digital Bits*. http://www.thedigitalbits.com/articles/cemadvdsales.html.

Chapin, Bill. "Box-Office Slump Has Theaters Reeling." *(Port Huron, MI) Times Herald*, September 25, 2005, A12A.

Cones, John W. *Dictionary of Film Finance and Distribution—a Guide for Independent Filmmakers*. Spokane, WA: Marquette Books, 2007.

———. *The Feature Film Distribution Deal—a Critical Analysis of the Single Most Important Film Industry Agreement*. Carbondale: Southern Illinois University Press, 1997.

———. *Film Industry Contracts*. Los Angeles: Self-published, 1993.

———. *43 Ways to Finance Your Feature Film: A Comprehensive Analysis of Film Finance*. 3rd ed. Carbondale: Southern Illinois University Press, 2008.

———. *Hollywood Wars—How Insiders Gained and Maintain Illegitimate Control over the Film Industry*. Spokane, WA: Marquette Books, 2007.

———. *Introduction to the Motion Picture Industry: A Guide for Filmmakers, Students, and Scholars*. Spokane, WA: Marquette Books, 2008.

Consolidated Management Group LLC v. the California Department of Corporations. 162 Cal. 4th 598 (2008).

Crowell, Thomas A. *The Pocket Lawyer for Filmmakers—a Legal Toolkit for Independent Producers*. Burlington, MA. Focal Press, 2007.

Davis, Peter. "Entry, Cannibalization and Bankruptcy in the U.S. Motion Picture Exhibition Market." Working paper. London School of Economics, 2003.

Dawtrey, Adam. "Study Has Faith in Global B.O. Bounce." *Variety.com*, January 4, 2006.

DeThomas, Arthur R., and Lin Grensing Pophal. *Writing a Convincing Business Plan*. Hauppage, NY: Barron's, 2001.

"DVD Frequently Asked Questions (and Answers)." *DVD Demystified*. http://dvddemystified.com/dvdfaq.html#1.9.

Dyson, Michael Eric. "Oscar Opens the Door." *Nation*, April 15, 2002.

Epstein, Edward Jay. "Downloading for Dollars—the Future of Hollywood Has Arrived." *Slate Magazine*, November 28, 2005.

Erickson, Gunnar, Harris Tulchin, and Mark Halloran. *The Independent Producer's Survival Guide—a Business and Legal Sourcebook*. 2nd ed. New York: Shirmer Trade Books, 2005.

Ford, Brian R., Jay M. Bonstein, and Patrick Preuitt. *The Ernst & Young Business Plan Guide*. New York: Ernst & Young, 2007.

"Foreign Grosses Rise to New Record." *Variety*, January 4, 2009.

Freshman, Elena R. "Commissions to Non-Broker/Dealers under California Law." *Beverly Hills Bar Journal* 22, no. 2 (Spring 1998).

Fritz, Ben. "Study: Web Piracy Costing Biz $850 Mil—Informa's Report First to Attach Figure to Growing Practice." *Variety.com*, January 27, 2005.

Garrett, Diane. "VHS, 30, Dies of Loneliness: The Home-Entertainment Format Lived a Fruitful Life." *Variety.com*, November 14, 2006.

Harris, Dana. "Pickup Pace Quickens." *Variety.com*, January 30, 2005.

Hettrick, Scott. "Spending on DVDs up 10%." *Variety.com*, December 29, 2005.

Holden v. Hagopian. 978 F2d. 1115 (9th Cir. 1992).

"Homevideo Biz Takes a Hit in '08." *Variety*, January 5, 2009.

"IFTA Membership International Sales Survey." *Independent Film & Television Alliance*, 2006. http://www.ifta.com.

Informa Media Group. "Film on the Internet." *informa*, January 2005. http://informa.com.

Jaeger, James. *The Movie Mogul Manual*. Devon, PA: Movie Pubs, 2007.

Kagan's MediaCast 2008. Paul Kagan Associates, Carmel, CA.

Kilday, Gregg. "AFM Books Record Number of Exhibitors." *Hollywood Reporter*, November 15, 2005.

———. "MPAA's "05 Scorecard: Box Office Slips, Costs Stabilize." *Hollywood Reporter*, March 10, 2006.

Lauzen, Martha M. "Celluloid Ceiling 2006 Report—Behind-the-Scenes Employment of Women in the Top 250 Films of 2005." PhD diss., San Diego State University, 2005.

Learmonth, Michael. "Aud Spending Spike—Surprise Hits Expected to Push B.O. Up 10%." *Variety.com*, August 1, 2004.

Lee, John, and Rob Holt. *The Producer's Business Handbook*. 2nd ed. Burlington, MA: Focal Press, 2006.

Levison, Louise. *Filmmakers and Financing—Business Plans for Independents*. 1998. Burlington, MA: Focal Press, 2007.

Loss, Louis, and Joel Seligman. *Fundamentals of Securities Regulation*. 4th ed. New York: Aspen, 2007.

Lytton, Christopher H. "Soft Money: The Weapon of Choice for the Runaway Productions." *Texas Entertainment and Sports Law Journal* 13, no. 1 (Spring 2004): 4–10. http://www.stcl.edu/txeslj/spring-2004.pdf.

Marcus, Adam J. "*Buchwald v. Paramount Pictures Corp.* and the Future of Net Profit." *Cardoza Arts & Entertainment Law Journal* 9, no. 2 (1991). http://www.cardozoaelj.net/i10.html.

McCarthy, Todd. "Sundance Stepping to an Int'l Rhythm." *Variety.com*, November 29, 2004.

McClintock, Pamela. "2007 Films Hit Record Box Office." *Variety*, January 2, 2008.

McClintock, Pamela, and Steven Zeitchik. "Sundance Deals Aplenty." *Variety.com*, January 25, 2007.

McKeever, Mike P. *How to Write a Business Plan*. Valencia, CA: Delta Printing Solutions, 2007.

McNary, Dave. "Filmmakers Can't Catch a Tax Break—California Incentives Bill Fails to Pass." *Variety.com*, September 4, 2006.

———. "Piracy Takes Broader Toll." *Variety.com*, October 2, 2006.

Mohr, Ian, and Pamela McClintock. "Sale Spree Hits Slopes." *Variety.com*, January 25, 2006. "Monster That Ate Hollywood, The." www.pbs.com, October 8, 2005.

Moore, Schuyler M. *The Biz: The Basic Business, Legal and Financial Aspects of the Film Industry*. Hollywood, CA: Silman-James Press, 2007.

Morfoot, Addie. "IFP Slates Projects for Feature Market." *Variety.com*, September 4, 2006.

Nemy, Philip. *Get a Reel Job*. Ventura, CA: Angel's Touch Productions, 1999.

O'Donnell, Pierce, and Dennis McDougal. *Fatal Subtraction—How Hollywood Really Does Business*. New York: Doubleday, 1992.

PricewaterhouseCoopers. *Global Entertainment and Media Outlook*. http://www.pwc.com/gx/en/global-entertainment-media-outlook/index.jhtml.

Prifti, William M. *Securities: Public and Private Offerings*. Rev. ed. Eagon, MN: Thomson, 1986.

"Production Pacts Get Dicey." *Variety.com*, August 6, 2006.

Ramer, Dan. "Blu-ray Disc Progress Report: Six Months after the Format War Victory." *DVDFile.com*, July 16, 2008. http://www.dvdfile.com/views/articles/25243-blu-ray-disc-progress-report.

Rosenfeld, Paul. *The Club Rules: Power, Money, Sex, and Fear—How It Works in Hollywood*. New York: Warner Books, 1992.

SEC v. Merchant Capital LLC. 483 F.3d 747 (11th Cir. 2007).

Sills, Steven D., and Ivan L. Axelrod. "Profit Participation in the Motion Picture Industry." *Los Angeles Lawyer* (April, 1989).

Snyder, Gabriel. "Icon Sez Regal Pulled Double-Cross." *Variety.com*, June 8, 2004.

Snyder, Gabriel, and Dana Harris. "Inside Move: Playing Hardball." *Variety.com*, June 13, 2004.

Stern, Matthew A. "Life in the Long Tail." *PopMatters*, July 6, 2006.

"Sundance Announces 2008 Lineup." *ShowBuzz*, November 29, 2007. www.showbuzz.cbsnews.com.

"Title Search Engine." *imdb*, 2006. www.imdbpro.com.

Tulchin, Harris E. "Selling Your Movie: The Role of the Producer's Representative." *Harris E. Tulchin*, 2000. http://www.medialawyer.com/REPART2.htm.

"2009 Sundance Film Festival Adds World Premiere of the Winning Season to Line Up." *Elites TV*, December 2008. http://www.elitestv.com/pub/2008/Dec/EEN495bd0359e656.html.

U.S. Department of Commerce. "The Migration of U.S. Film & Television Production." Study on Runaway Production. Washington, DC: U.S. Dept. of Commerce, March 2001. http://www.ita.doc.gov/media/migration11901.pdf.

"US Movie Market Summary 1995–2009." *Nash Information Services*. http://www.the-numbers.com/market.

U.S. Securities and Exchange Commission. Item 10(d), section 228, 17 CFR.

VSDA—2003 Annual Report on the Home Entertainment Industry. http://www.vsda.org/.

Weisman, Eric. "Hollywood's Ethical Malaise." *Variety.com*, October 12, 2004.

Williamson v. Tucker. 645 F.2d 404 (5th Cir. 1981).

Index

John W. Cones, a securities/entertainment attorney in California, is the author of seven books relating to the U.S. film industry, including *43 Ways to Finance Your Feature Film* (3rd ed., 2007). He teaches legal and business affairs classes in Los Angeles area film schools and lectures regularly at film-industry organizations and universities throughout the country.